IN AN INSTANT

STORIES OF RESILIENCE AND COURAGE

KIM MOONEY

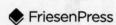 FriesenPress

One Printers Way
Altona, MB R0G 0B0
Canada

www.friesenpress.com

Cover by thoughtshop.com

Klutch Photography
klutchphotography.com

ISBN
978-1-03-831258-7 (Hardcover)
978-1-03-831257-0 (Paperback)
978-1-03-831259-4 (eBook)

1. *SELF-HELP, DEATH, GRIEF, BEREAVEMENT*

Distributed to the trade by The Ingram Book Company

To Bob & Lil,
Thank you so very
much for the love,
care & support you've
shown to Greg and me. I
pray as you read these
stories of courage & resilience,
they will help you through
your own lives'
difficult times. With love,
Judy.

Dedication:

To my mother.
Relentlessly optimistic
Steadfast and determined
Until the very end of her life.

To my storytellers
For trusting me

By Kim Mooney:
Hidden Daughter-Secret Sisters; A Story of Adoption

OUTLINE

ACKNOWLEDGEMENTS

NO BOOK IS EVER WRITTEN ALONE. I had an idea, but it was the storytellers who opened their hearts to me and shared their stories that made the book whole. Together we wove their memories into chapters, and at the end of each chapter, you understood what it means to be resilient in the face of instant and catastrophic loss.

A most special thank you to my friend Greg, who was the spark for this book. His courage, humour, and faith were my inspiration. There would be no story without you, Greg. You will live in my heart forever. *Loved you then. Love you now. Love you forever.*

To Diane, Dodie, Bindy, Sharon and Paul, Liz, Shawna, and Judy — thank you for trusting me to tell your story with gentleness and compassion.

To my editor Audrey McClellan — thank you. You kept me focused and helped me bring these stories to life. Your encouragement, kindness, and gentle approach helped me keep going during the long days of COVID-19.

To Jennifer Gunning — thank you for being my first editor and for sharing this writing journey from beginning to end. You believed I had something important to share, and that was what I remembered on the "stuck" days. It always made the difference between a blank page and a full one.

To Mel McLeod and Julie Holder — thank you for reading draft after draft. You were my cheering squad. Having you out there, just an email away—what a gift!

To Dina Stoddard — thank you for your willingness to step into uncharted territory!

And finally, to Chad — thank you for always urging me to take the time and space I needed to write. You are the love of my life. As E.E. Cummings says, *I carry your heart, I carry it in my heart.*

FOREWORD

THE IDEA FOR THIS BOOK, *IN AN INSTANT: Stories of Resilience and Courage,* came to me in 2019, but books take time to move from dreams to reality, and by the time I finished, the world had plunged into, and slowly emerged from, a pandemic. Resilience was needed by everyone, everywhere.

The people who told their stories in this book were chosen because of trauma that created instantaneous life changes for them. The stories are about their resilience during the months and years that followed those life-changing events. But the interviews for the book all happened after COVID-19 arrived. Each of the participants asked me if I was going to talk about the impact of the pandemic because this book, my book, was about resilience—people's stories about personal grit. They wanted me to tell everyone that life throws curves when we least expect them, and for us, in this time of our lives, COVID-19 was the biggest curve yet. They wanted everyone to know what they learned: you can go on even when you are not sure how.

At first I said no. I knew that hundreds of amazing stories about resilience would emerge from the pandemic, but I knew that would be someone else's book, not mine. The more I thought about it, though, the more I knew that I did have to talk about the pandemic, at least for a moment, because you will read two stories in my book in which people were very impacted by COVID-19. You will understand how as you read.

To write a book about resilience in the years clouded by a pandemic feels like a blessing in disguise. I will tell you nine stories about nine remarkable people. And in the years to come you will read many stories about people from every corner of the world who will carry the imprint of this extraordinary and gruesome time in history. As you read those stories, you will remember reading about my nine friends and hear their words reminding everyone that resilience comes when you least expect it and when you need it most.

"It is no use going back to yesterday,
Because I was a different person then."
Lewis Carroll

INTRODUCTION

I STOOD QUIETLY, LOOKING OUT the window on a Thursday morning in May 2018. The sky was clear and bright, that crystal-clear blue we so rarely get on the West Coast. Not a cloud in the sky. As I took a sip of my tea, the air filled with the scream of sirens. The shrill sound of the fire trucks and ambulance drew closer and closer.

Suddenly the vehicles were in front of my house. They stopped, lights flashing. Men were jumping from the vehicles before they completely stopped, running toward the house directly across the street. I froze in my spot and watched, fascinated in the moment by these running action figures. Within minutes they were back on the sidewalk.

In that instant I knew something bad had happened. I ran. Two paramedics loaded my neighbour into the ambulance. A third paramedic straddled him on the gurney and furiously pumped his chest, not stopping for a moment. The doors of the ambulance slammed shut, and it raced away. Sirens were shrieking once again. As his wife stumbled through her door, tears streaming down her face, I grabbed her and, with my arms around her, gently guided her, half holding, half pushing, into another neighbour's car. They too raced away. I stood watching, nothing more to do.

She came home later. He didn't. He was gone and she was left to figure out how to live without him after more than forty years of being together. As I once again gazed at the brilliant blue sky, I wondered, "Now what? What will she do? How will she move forward? *Will* she move forward?"

Over the following months I watched her lurch ahead, day in, day out, trying to make sense of her new life. She didn't want a new life, but no one had asked her. It began anyway.

From time to time, I see glimmers of the person I knew the day before that gloriously sunny one in May 2018. Then I see the light in her dwindle, dim, as if the fog is rolling in, rolling over her, and she sinks. The next time, she emerges from the fog for a few moments longer than the time before. I see her slowly making her way in her new life.

I have known others who faced similar tragedy and never really recovered. They seem all right in passing, mowing the lawn or getting the groceries, but when I dig a little deeper, I see that they are fundamentally broken. A fog has settled on their shoulders like a heavy mantle, and it never moves, never shifts. And I wonder, "What is it that makes the difference? Why do some people step into life once again and others remain on the sidelines, lingering as if simply waiting for their turn to die?"

As these questions rolled around in my head, I was drawn back to my teaching days. I was teaching a class about our capacity for change, how we can prepare ourselves to be nimble in the face of the unknown. The sessions always created great debate, something I enjoyed. But sometimes I would veer off script and introduce the concept of resilience. I asked my students what their experience with resilience was like, and these conversations provided us with hours of discussion. There were stories of triumph over the harsh realities of living through difficult times, and there were just as many stories of the inability of some to thrive in the face of disaster. There was Elan's story of being driven from her home in a small African country to find herself in Canada, homeless, penniless. And yet here she was, studying for her master's degree. How did she find the strength to endure the hardships thrown at her? And Kevin, a middle-aged farmer from western Canada, who lost everything because he drank too much and yet found his footing once again. How? And what of those who didn't find their way back? There was Jackie's story. She came from the North, a harsh and isolated place. She told us that many in her community felt hopeless, unable to make positive changes in their lives. Her young nephew was a casualty of that loss of all hope. He saw no way to improve his life in the community, and in a moment of great anguish he took his own life. I was often left wondering what role hope played in our ability to be resilient. So many stories, so many different results.

In 2019 I decided to write a book, one that would tell the stories of the resilient people in my life. It was important to me that the stories were not seen as simply anecdotal. I wanted to show how they reflected what the literature said about resilience. So I turned to the experts, those who studied the concept of resilience and who wrestled with the same questions my students and I posed for each other. What role did resilience have in helping people like my storytellers carry on in the face of tragedy? Are you born with a resilient gene that sits in the background just in case you need it? Can you develop resilience like you develop skills in accounting or skating? I just didn't know.

Resilience has become a topic of much interest over the last couple of decades. You can find any number of articles in popular magazines that will tell you how to build your own resilience, a proactive approach in case you encounter adversity. Some articles outline four steps to improve resilience; others are seven-step plans. All have good ideas. The underlying assumption in many of these articles is that we are all capable of building our resilience muscles if we focus on certain aspects of life, like building a strong support system, having a spiritual or religious base, or being optimistic about what life can hold for you. I don't disagree with the premise because these parts of our lives are important, but who knowingly rehearses the four or the seven steps just in case they need them? My neighbour was busy living her life when her world crashed. I am pretty sure she hadn't been practising a four-step resilience program just in case she needed it.

When I was a student I chose mathematics as my major area for study, and I did a minor in literature. Math was a huge challenge, so I used English literature as my refuge. One of the books I discovered was Victor Frankl's *Man's Search for Meaning*. Frankl was a world-renowned psychiatrist and a survivor of the Nazi death camps. It was an extraordinary book and the story stayed with me for many years. When I began my review of works about resilience, his was the one I went to first.

At its core, *Man's Search for Meaning* is a story of resilience. When asked why he wrote the book, Frankl said, "I wanted simply to convey to the readers by way of a concrete example that life holds a potential meaning under any circumstance, even the most miserable ones" (p.

xiv). He believed in the power of hope. I see hope in the people who shared their stories with me. Each of them had the will to go forward, to live for something yet unknown.

Harold Kushner, a well-known American rabbi, wrote the foreword for the 2006 edition of Frankl's book. In the foreword, Kushner quotes the philosopher Friedrich Nietzsche: "He who has a *Why* to live for can bear the *How*." Kushner recognized that Frankl's experience of suffering in Auschwitz reinforced what was already one of his key ideas: "Life is not primarily a quest for pleasure, as Freud believed, or a quest for power, as Alfred Adler (psychotherapist) taught, but a quest for meaning. The greatest task for any person is to find meaning in his or her life" (p. x). Kushner reminds us that we can't always control what happens to us, but we can choose how to respond. This was a key factor for the people who shared their stories with me. It also reminded me of times in my life when unexpected events occurred and I had to decide what path I would take. I couldn't change what happened, but I did control how I would respond. Kushner was as fascinated with Frankl's ideas as I was, echoing my question: is the choice of *how* you move forward in life the seed of resilience regardless of *what* has happened?

In his book *Good to Great*, Jim Collins refers to the Stockdale Paradox, which describes how a person can hold two opposing ideas at once: accepting the reality of a difficult situation and, at the same time, imagining a better one. Facts and faith merge to create a new picture. Collins named this concept after US Admiral James Stockdale, who was the highest-ranking US military officer held as a prisoner of war in the Vietnam War. He was a prisoner for eight years in a brutal environment and he survived. What kept him going? Stockdale said, "You must never confuse faith that you will prevail in the end—which you can never afford to lose—with the discipline to confront the most brutal facts of your current reality, whatever they might be" (p. 85). Realistic faith, perhaps?

Both Frankl and Stockdale lived through horrendous experiences. They told their stories not to frighten readers but to give them hope. Their words were a conduit, a platform to tell the world that even when terrible things happen to us, something better, something good could emerge. If we can accept *what* has happened, perhaps we will then find our own path to how we can live a full life despite the current situation. They reminded me that finding a new path that holds meaning is resilience in action. And it is seldom, if ever, easy. As psychologist Maria Konnikova wrote, "If you are lucky enough to never experience any sort of adversity, we won't know how resilient you are. It's only when you're faced with obstacles, stress, and other environmental threats that resilience, or the lack of it, emerges. Do you succumb or do you surmount?"[1] Every storyteller you will meet in this book asked themselves that question at some point in their journey: "Do I give up or do I go forward?" It may have been just a momentary thought, or it may have been a daily struggle to answer, "What will I do?" Each person chose "surmount."

Frankl, Stockdale, and Konnikova's beliefs about resilience were echoed by Diane Coutu. Coutu, a business consultant and former senior editor for *Harvard Business Review* (HBR), wrote a seminal article about resilience called "How Resilience Works" for HBR.[2] She wanted to know why some people endure great hardship and find a way forward. Believing it to be resilience, she asked, "What exactly is that quality of resilience that carries people through life?" She concludes, "Resilience is something you realize after the fact." This made complete sense to me.

She reminds us that when we ask the question "Why me?" during very difficult times, we need to turn it around and ask "Why not me?" Terrible things happen; most often we are not responsible for them. But we are responsible for what we do next, and that is what matters. That is where our resilience counts. Even when we don't know how to begin again, how to leave despair and reach for hope, we have to trust, to believe that life still holds meaning.

Coutu says the ability to maintain a sense of optimism is a fundamental aspect of resilience, but at the same time, we must accept the reality of the situation. She adds, "Facing reality, really facing it, is gruelling work" (p. 7). Frankl and Stockdale believed that this was key to their survival. They both said that prisoners who didn't face the reality of their situation died.

---

1   Maria Konnikova, "How People Learn to Become Resilient," *The New Yorker*, February 11, 2016.

2   Diane Coutu, "How Resilience Works," *Harvard Business Review*, May 2002.

When you can find a balance between the reality of your situation and optimism for the future, a renewed purpose and meaning for life emerges. Coutu goes on to say, "Resilient people build bridges from present-day hardships to a fuller, better constructed future" (p. 9). This seems impossible to imagine during tragedy. But Frankl did it. Stockdale did it. The people you will meet in this book did it.

Coutu talks about one additional feature of resilience that intrigued me, building on an idea expressed by Frankl and Stockdale. She says that, over time, resilient people look at their broken life and figure out what pieces can be mended and what must be left behind. I think this is a difficult concept to grasp until you have lived through it. Even then, I suspect it is much more of a subconscious act.

Thankfully most of us have very little practice living through traumatic events. But when they do happen, we are at a loss. How we go on becomes the challenge, and it all takes so much energy. Yet even when their energy is at its lowest, resilient people will search for ways to go forward. I am reminded of Leonard Cohen's song "Anthem" (1992) when he reminds us that light finds its way through cracks, sometimes showing us a pathway that we would have otherwise, missed.

The literature suggests that resilience is real, yet it remains difficult to define explicitly. You may be born resilient, or you may need to learn it along the way, or maybe it is both innate and learned. Maybe it doesn't really matter, because until you need to draw on that inner grit, wherever it comes from, it will lie dormant. You might not know you are resilient until you need to be, and even then, the minutes, the hours, the days— they are hard. But no matter what, you can't go back to the day *before*. And standing still is not an option. Time moves us all along.

Families often have stories that are repeated so often they become more like folklore than fact. We had them in our family, and when I thought about one particular story, I realized, "Ah, this is a clear depiction of what being resilient means." I may have difficulty defining resilience, but I know it when I see it, and I saw it in this story. The family tale belongs to my mother, one of the most resilient people I have ever known.

She was born in Saskatoon, Saskatchewan, and she lived in the same house until she was twenty-two years old. To hear her talk, she had a fairy-tale childhood filled with picnics, swimming, skating, parties, and boys. She was a happy, carefree person who believed that life would always be good to her. When she was twenty-two, she went on a blind date and met the love of her life. He was a pilot in the Royal Canadian Air Force. She described him as handsome, funny, and kind. He was older than her, worldly. Every time she described him, she used the same words, with the emphasis on *handsome*.

She loved him instantly and for the rest of her life. She loved him until she died at age ninety-eight in 2018. But he died on November 7, 1943. He was only twenty-seven years old. He died in an airplane crash over the English Channel, and his body was never recovered. The last time she saw him was in the spring of 1943, when she took a train from Saskatoon to Halifax to see him before he left for England. She wanted to say goodbye, but more importantly, she wanted to tell him she was pregnant. As far as she was concerned, her fairy-tale life was right on track. She had a handsome husband and a baby due in December. Perfect. Except on November 7, he was gone. In an instant, her perfect life changed forever.

Nothing was as she dreamed it would be. Dreams shattered around her like a crystal goblet sliding off the table to the stone floor below. But she had to pick up some of those glass shards and step over others. She had to find a way to keep living because she had a baby on the way. And because, well, what else could she do? Slowly, very slowly, she began to move through the grief that engulfed her every day.

She had no one to help her figure out how to navigate the grief. She was forbidden to talk about her dead husband. Her mother told her not to talk about her "sadness," to just move on. She told me that the grief was so intense that there were times when she didn't think she could take another breath. But she had to. She had to figure out how to live without him. The baby came, a beautiful blond boy who looked just like his father. She had to keep living but she didn't know how to do that. Looking backward every day to the lost life wasn't an option but moving forward seemed impossible too. Miraculously, she chose to re-engage with life, taking her deep love for that man with her.

Lots of days she cast her eyes back, wishing for that other life. She was haunted by the fact that no body was returned to her. She could trick herself into believing that maybe, just maybe, it was a big mistake. He would come home. She dreamed about him all the time, catching glimpses of him on street corners, at parties, in all sorts of odd places. But then, like a puff of smoke, he disappeared again. She married for a second time, brought two more children into the fold, and moved on. She endured different trauma and pain in her life, but that never stopped her from living a full life. And why? Because she was resilient, she was irrepressible, she was tough. She was one of the most optimistic, tenacious people I knew. Where did that come from? I am not sure, and she isn't here anymore for me to ask. But without ever putting a name to it, her resilience became a beacon of hope for me when I faced life-altering, crashing loss. Her spirit still carries me.

And so, with the spirit of my mother sitting on my shoulders and the memory of my neighbour's experience echoing in my mind, I wanted to share stories of others I have known who faced instant loss and yet found a way back to a new life. Each of them grieves still, and yet they live with hope.

The people you will meet in this book are resilient. Like my mother, they are ordinary people living their lives in the best way they know how. They aren't famous or wealthy. They are what one friend calls "just plain folk." But they embody the spirit I saw in my mother and my neighbour. Each of them expressed surprise when I told them I was writing a book about resilient people and wanted to include their stories. "Why?" they asked. "Because you are my definition of resilient," I said. None of the storytellers defined themselves as resilient until we talked about it. Even then, they weren't sure the term applied to them. They believed that they were simply getting on with the task of life.

Like my mother and my neighbour, they experienced traumatic change in their lives, change that happened in one moment. These are stories about what happened to them and how they navigated the days, months, and years after. There were many moments, many days, when they slid backward, overcome by the tragedy that changed the course of their lives. But they kept moving and their lives are now full, hopeful. I wanted to understand why; what propelled them onward in spite of the overwhelming desire to give up and give in, to stand still? And I wanted to know who they were now because they embraced their new life.

You will meet men and women, including two married couples. You will read about cancer, death of a spouse, death of a child, and grave illness. The stories have common threads, yet at the same time, each is unique. You will hear the voices of the storytellers, feel their pain, and see them emerge from grief. None of them have forgotten the day their lives changed forever, but they have found a way to live with their loss and, at the same time, live fully. You will come to feel their spirits and, hopefully, see them as I do. Strong, fierce, extraordinary. Resilient.

CHAPTER ONE: DIANE

Kim's Story

I MET DIANE IN AUGUST 1988. *She was a brand-new graduate of the Child and Youth Care undergraduate program at the University of Victoria in Victoria, BC. We were both new members of the Child Life staff at BC Children's Hospital in Vancouver. Child Life specialists are responsible for the psycho-social needs of sick children. They help children, youth, and families cope with stressors related to illness, hospitalization, trauma, and loss. It is an emotionally taxing job, and Diane was perfect for the work. I worked on the Pediatric Oncology (Childhood Cancer) unit and Diane worked on the Adolescent unit. She was young, enthusiastic—full of ideas and ideals. Exuberant. She had a marvellous sense of humour and immediately immersed herself in all aspects of hospital life, both clinical and social.*

She was equally social outside the hospital, and we all waited anxiously for Monday morning coffee breaks to hear about the latest weekend escapades. One morning in the summer of 1989, Diane arrived with the biggest smile yet. She had met a guy. His name was Jeff. He was an ironworker by trade but supplemented his income as the doorman at a neighbourhood bar. We all leaned in as she described this tall, handsome man. Jeff was the friend of a friend and was sneaking Diane and her friends into the bar. He let them in one at a time, giving Diane time to chat with him. By the time the evening was over, she was smitten!

Diane and Jeff started dating, and this new relationship moved forward quickly. Morning coffee time at the hospital was filled with Jeff. I felt I knew him long before we met. They dated for a while, and then in 1993 were married. It was a magical time in Di's life. She had the perfect job and the perfect man. What could go wrong?

Diane's enthusiasm for life has seldom wavered, but it was put to a crushing test when Jeff died as the result of a car accident on September 18, 1997. Life as Diane knew it stopped that day. But she drew on her life experience to help herself during and after that difficult time. She reflected as she went along on how to live fully again—how not to be a victim. She lost herself for moments along the way, but she found deep pools of inner strength and used them to move back toward equilibrium. She was strong enough to accept help when she needed it and to trust that those around her would carry her through dark and confusing times. Diane's resilient nature was born of many things. This is her story.

Diane's Story

It was September 18, 1997. My phone rang at 6:20 a.m. The day stands out even more vividly for me because, with one of my colleagues, I was supposed to be launching an exciting new initiative that morning for transitioning pediatric patients into adult care. We were working with several teams at the hospital, and we had a big presentation that morning. There was a ripple effect because of what happened. I had to tell my colleague why I wasn't able to be with her for the presentation, but I suspect I wasn't very coherent on the phone. Word got out at the hospital that there had been some kind of accident, but the details were sketchy. All of the Child Life specialists were gathered in the office, waiting for the director of the program, and I was notably absent. It was described to me later that there was silent panic in the room as everyone believed it was me who had been in an accident. Then all the feelings of relief quickly dissolved into immense sadness when they learned that it was Jeff who had died.

The 6:20 a.m. phone call was from a physician in the Intensive Care unit at Foothills Hospital in Calgary. He told me that Jeff had been in a car accident. At that point he was still alive, but, they told me, he had a severe brain injury and it was very serious. I don't know if the doctor actually said to me "He's not expected to live" or if I leapt to that conclusion on my own. Regardless, the doctor said, "You need to come now." I needed to get to Calgary. That whole conversation with the doctor was pretty surreal. It was the first of many surreal conversations. I hung the phone up at 6:27 a.m.—in seven minutes my entire life changed.

Jeff had just bought a new Jeep Grand Cherokee—his first new vehicle ever, and I'll say "his pride and joy," because I'm sure he used those words! He was going to Calgary to work on a movie. Did I mention Jeff was an actor? This shy guy with a stutter throughout school decided one day to pursue acting. He got an acting coach, he had head shots done and created a beautiful portfolio, and he found an agent. He landed commercials, a few roles as an extra in TV and movies, and some parts in local theatre. The movie in Calgary was exciting—it was a small cast and he would have a prominent role. The director was a student at Emily Carr, the Vancouver art school. So although it was a local production, it was another role to add to Jeff's resumé.

When he planned his trip to Calgary, Jeff wasn't going to take his new vehicle. He was meant to go with someone else, but he changed his mind at the last moment and drove his new Jeep—he couldn't help himself. He was gone before I got home from work. I called my mom that night and told her I had this horrible feeling about him driving. It was like a wave went through me. I can't explain it.

And now here I was, home alone and trying to figure out what to do first. I remember thinking, "I don't know how to book a flight, to even get dressed, and I don't know what to take with me." I didn't know if I was going to end up staying there and if so, for how long. All these things, these practical things, were going through my head at the same time. I couldn't figure out what to do about any of them. I called my girlfriend Leah and she came over. Leah made the plane reservation for me because I didn't remember how to dial the number. I called her but I couldn't seem to work the phone anymore. She helped me call my parents and Jeff's mom and his sister. She also helped me call my colleague at the hospital. I said that she had to go ahead and do the presentation without me. I think I probably said all kinds of stupid things to everyone. I just don't know.

I remember leaving the house without showering, with mismatched socks and a purple shirt that I hated wearing because Leah picked it out for me. But I didn't know how to get dressed by myself, so I didn't argue with her. And I was so grateful for her help. She had a newborn son, but yet she was able to figure out a way to come with me to Calgary. I know all those things happened, but I don't really know how they happened. We got on the plane. I know the flight attendant was really kind. She knew we were flying for compassionate reasons, and at some point I blurted out that my husband was dying. She said very nice things to me, but I couldn't really tell you what she said. She brought a box of tissues for Leah and me, and she took one herself as we all cried together. There were lots of surreal moments like this along the way.

When we arrived at the hospital, Leah and I went to the intensive care unit (ICU) waiting room and a social worker was waiting for us. I remember thinking, "Wait a minute, that's usually my job. I'm the one that usually works with families in difficult times." My second or perhaps simultaneous thought was, "It's bad . . . they don't send a social worker unless it's bad." But everything about this situation was wrong.

The social worker told me Jeff had died a half hour before I arrived. In the time it took me to get to Calgary, he had died. Leah stayed in the waiting room, and the social worker took me into the room where Jeff was lying. He looked like he was sleeping. I had to know that this really was Jeff because I just couldn't believe it. I did irrational things like checking his birthmarks to make sure it was him, and then I knew it really was him. He was dead. At some point I also saw Jeff's sister, who had arrived in Calgary from Vancouver before me. I remember feeling jealous—possessive. I don't know the exact feeling, but it seemed unfair that she got to see him before I did. I had no right to feel that way, but I did.

I don't how long I was in the hospital, maybe a few hours. At one point I went into the bathroom by myself, and people were very worried. They kept shouting for me. I finally said, "I really am just peeing—it's okay." Finally we left the hospital, went to the airport, and flew home.

I don't know how I did this. Leah arranged it all. These were the kinds of things that happened around me that day and for many days ahead. It was remarkable.

My mom and dad were already in Vancouver and in my apartment when I got home, and my cousin was on her way. I remember thinking, "It is 'my' apartment now, not 'our' apartment." In those early hours and days, I had so many thoughts about what I had lost that brought on fresh tears each time.

The memories of the first two days are ingrained in my head. Everybody wanted to know how they could help, asking what I needed. What did I need? I didn't know what I needed. Except I needed my husband. Suddenly I was a thirty-two-year-old without a husband. I needed him. So people just started to do things, concrete things. Jeff had just bought a motorcycle and my oldest brother, Doug, took it back to the dealership. The hospital where I worked organized food for our family—lots and lots of food. My dad took me to the bank because I dreaded telling complete strangers I was a widow. People did very practical things. Good things. And some offered a variety of advice, most of which I either didn't need or couldn't understand in that moment. I realized I didn't want to be in Vancouver, close to all these caring people. I needed to get away from the kindness and the questions. But I needed to wait until after the funeral.

Jeff died four days before my thirty-second birthday. The day before the funeral I got a phone call from a store, asking me if I would be home to accept a delivery. The clerk very excitedly told me that my husband had picked out a beautiful piece of furniture I had wanted and asked for it to be delivered around my birthday. I sobbed into the phone that he must be mistaken, my husband was dead, and handed the phone over to my mom. As it turned out, Jeff had ordered the piece weeks in advance. When it was delivered, I thought my heart would never heal from the pain.

My mom and dad took me to the funeral home. We arranged for the funeral to be in the same church we got married in. I had lost a ton of weight even in the four or five days since he died, so I didn't have a dress that fit me. My friend Kathy brought me over several "widow appropriate" (dark and past the knee) dresses because the thought of shopping for a new outfit to wear to my husband's funeral was more than I could bear. As I stood in the wings, waiting for the funeral to begin, I had this huge reaction to somebody coming in the wrong door of the church and seeing me before I was ready to be seen. I was furious, and after, I remember so regretting my insane behaviour. But I'm sure I was cut a little bit of slack.

My dear friends and colleagues from the hospital made the funeral program and all of the food for the funeral reception. Four hundred people came to the service. They came from all walks of Jeff's life. Throughout it all I was still trying to be a hostess. There were so many people in attendance, and I was so humbled that they had come to the funeral just to support me. So many colleagues from work that I remember wondering who was left at the hospital; relatives that I hadn't seen in years; friends of friends that I had met briefly who just wanted to pay their respects. All for me. It was like receiving the biggest hug. I felt very cared for, and I remember my mom saying, "It makes it easier for your dad and me to leave you, knowing you have so many people that care about you." And she was right.

After the funeral there was going to be one reception at the church, and then Jeff's mom wanted a separate reception outside the church—something more casual and an opportunity for those who knew Jeff (many "before my time") to talk about him and celebrate his life. At that point I didn't care. I was a zombie. Besides, it was my duty to be a good hostess, and that meant accommodating whatever gatherings people told me to have. Truth was, I didn't care about anything other than to get through the day.

The second reception took place later that afternoon. I can't recall when I found out that the group of actors from Emily Carr who were with Jeff in Calgary would be in attendance. I was told the director of the film would be there as well. He was the driver of Jeff's vehicle. The man who didn't see a bend in the road and drove off course. The man who killed the person in the passenger seat, my husband. The man who lived while my husband died. I know I talked to the group of actors—but the director didn't attend after all. He was still recovering from his injuries. I was told he said he was devasted and remorseful. They told me that his acting friends had set up a small memorial for Jeff in their building at Emily Carr on Granville Island. At the time I was too numb to know exactly how I felt about hearing any of those things.

My family was concerned about my emotional well-being, and they set up a protective wall around me during the reception. Finally, at one point in the afternoon, my brother came over to me and said, "We're going now. You're done. You have to stop this." And I said, "What do you mean I'm done?" In any other setting I was always the social butterfly. It was no different that day. I was making sure everyone else was doing okay despite the toll it was taking on me, which, apparently, I failed to recognize. But I had learned over the course of the previous few days that others had my best interests at heart. So I listened. And we left.

After the funeral I went home to Terrace (a small town in northern BC) with my parents for about three weeks. In that time many other tragedies happened in my family. My dad's sister died; my sister's father-in-law died. I had a little bunny named Squish who I had farmed out to somebody, and he got very sick. My cousin in Langley had a brain aneurysm. I remember thinking, "Hey, God. Come on—cut a girl a little slack here." My mom and dad went to Edmonton for my sister's father-in-law's funeral, leaving me alone for about four or five days. A week or so after they got back my mom said, "I don't know why we left you like that." She was so filled with regret. That was an example of what was happening all around me. Everybody was unsure what to do for me, with me. I told her that I didn't mind being left alone. I needed that little bit of breathing room. But she was still filled with remorse.

And being home with my parents was good. Home is home is home—it was familiar. Life revolved around our kitchen table. People would come to me, sit with me. Mom and Dad's friends and a few of my friends that still lived there came. I would get up in the morning; Mom and Dad and I would have our coffee and, quite often, have a little cry. Then people just came. It had always been like that at Mom and Dad's house, so it was very comforting to me. We tidied up the garden, did normal things. I needed my own time too, and they were so respectful of what I needed. Lots of crying and the "what am I going to do next?" question. We even talked about planning a holiday. Lots and lots of talking.

Sleep was challenging. I wasn't a great sleeper even before Jeff died, but it was really hard after. So I slept whenever sleep came. I loved to go to sleep because Jeff would often be in my dreams. He also visited in other ways. He had ways of letting us know that he was watching us. He did this with lots of people, but particularly with my mom. She would hear him sing her favourite church hymn, which was funny because he didn't sing to her when he was alive!

When Jeff was alive, he used to ring our friends' doorbells and then hide. After he died, he still rang their doorbells. Many people told me their doorbells would ring but no one was there, and then they knew— it was Jeff. Even my mom and dad's doorbell would ring. I loved those stories. We all got such comfort from his antics . . . and we could laugh when it didn't feel like there was much to laugh about. It was interesting telling people that Jeff would appear—it spooked some people when I told them, but others completely related and had similar ghost-like stories to tell of their beloved family member. I also would have lots and lots of visions of him. I got so much comfort from them, and when they stopped, I remember thinking, "Well bloody hell, that's not fair." I missed him so much.

At the end of the three weeks, I left Terrace. My cousin who had the aneurysm was still in hospital, but her mom (my aunt) had come to help my cousin's husband. I moved into their house in Langley as well. I moved in on the premise that they needed my help. I was most comfortable with being a caregiver. I didn't want to be the receiver anymore. Or at least not for a while. But in hindsight, I believe I needed them more than they needed me. After about ten days, I knew it was time to finally go home. My home, the one without Jeff.

There were so many opinions about whether or not I should stay in the apartment Jeff and I owned. I couldn't understand why people wanted me to move, except to say, "It must be so painful to live there without Jeff." It was quite the opposite. We bought our condo before many of our friends were purchasing property, and we were proud to be homeowners. We had done some renovations, had purchased real, grown-up furniture, and had added Squish, the bunny, to our family. It was my home, and I quite defiantly told anyone who suggested I should move that I had no intention of leaving. What I did accept was my brother's help with packing up Jeff's clothes. I couldn't bear to give them away at the time, so he helped me take them to my girlfriend's, who agreed to temporarily store them. And I did do a kitchen renovation about a year later, since the 1970s cupboards and countertops were in desperate need of updating. Otherwise, it was a home full of memories that I had no desire to leave, and I know in hindsight it was the best decision.

After I left my cousin's, I did go back to work part-time. I had been off for two months and I decided I was okay, I could return. I continued my work on the Transition project that I had abruptly left the day Jeff died. This meant I was not working directly with children and families. I was so grateful for that because I wasn't sure how I was going to keep my shit together in front of families. Many of the adolescent patients I had been working with before the Transition project had cystic fibrosis. I couldn't fathom going through an end-of-life scenario with them and their families. The Transition project was very task oriented, giving me that necessary distance from the emotional requirements of direct patient care. Except it didn't insulate me from my own emotional distress. I tried to keep it all under control. I think I went on autopilot.

During this time I decided that I had to stop grieving. I just had to stop. That's all there was to it. I had gone to a grief support group and ended up comparing my situation to everyone else's. Mine came up short. I thought, "Jeff and I had been together for nine and a half years but look at these couples who have been married for fifty years. Look at this parent whose child has died. Look at this person who lost a sibling fifteen years ago and is still in immense pain and grief." I thought, "Snap out of it, girl, just get on with it." So I decided—no more grieving. Check. Done. Except it had only been three months. How could I have possibly expected to just "get on with it" after only three months?

I wanted everything to feel "normal." I didn't like being sad every single moment of every single day. And when I did have glimpses of happiness, that didn't feel right either. How could I be happy when my husband was dead? And why wouldn't people bring up his name? Oh yes, it was too painful to talk about. So I thought, "Keep it all inside, keep moving, get over it, get on with it." That's what I was supposed to do. I was going to be the model grieving widow. Get me through Kübler-Ross's stages of grief so I could show the world I was the textbook griever.[3]

I somehow managed to work throughout 1998. I'm not sure how productive I was nor how my colleagues would have truly described my level of coping. However, having that routine gave me some purpose and I was grateful to have something to concentrate on besides the emptiness I was feeling. But as the year was coming to an end, I felt myself beginning to unravel. Truthfully, I completely and utterly lost it. It scared the hell out of me. I wasn't the pillar of strength I desperately wanted to be. I wasn't sleeping. I thought that retail therapy would help and so I shopped endlessly, only to take it all back days later. I remember thinking people should be able to read my mind and know what I wanted or needed, which more and more often was to be left to my own devices. I think I looked like the perfect grieving widow to the outside world, that maybe I was actually okay. But I wasn't. I just wanted to be my old self. But *she* was gone, and I was lost.

At this same time that I could feel myself falling apart, our Transition project was at a crossroads for funding and I was going to have to go back to clinical work. I walked into my boss's office and said, "I need a year. I am done here. I just can't do this. I cannot come into clinical work." She said, "I don't want to put a timeline on it. You've got the time; do what you need to do. But let's not put an end time on it. Let's check in along the way and see how you're doing." That's when Mom, Dad, and I went on the vacation we had planned at the kitchen table in the first weeks after Jeff died.

In December 1998, we went to the Cook Islands and Hawai'i for six weeks. My parents, as always, were my pillars of support. We did a lot together but they always gave me time and space when I needed it. I know a number of people we met at the resort questioned what a girl in her early thirties was doing travelling with her parents. My parents had a polite but curt response of "She's gone through a recent challenging

---

3   In her book *On Death and Dying*, psychiatrist Elisabeth Kübler-Ross introduced a model that described five stages many people go through when they are given a terminal diagnosis. The model was soon applied to grief.

time" and left it up to me if I wanted to elaborate. If I did, the pitying looks were more than I could stand, so I often left people wondering what challenge I faced. I'm sure more than a few thought I was a recovering drug addict, but I didn't care. During those weeks together I became very close to my parents; I would later describe my mom as my confidante, my rock, and my strength. She instinctively knew what I needed, and that remained throughout our lives together.

Shortly after I got home, I left again. I went to the South of France for a month. I flew to France with a friend of Jeff's who had relatives there but didn't see him again until the day we flew back home. I needed to escape. I needed to be alone. I needed to know I could navigate in a different country on my own. I'm not sure why, but exercising this independence was very important to me. I stayed in three different cities and managed to make my way around without any problems. But I did have a bit of a safety net. My friend and colleague Anna and her husband were staying in a neighbouring city. I saw them a few times while I was in Cannes.

One afternoon, Anna and I took a ferry over to a small island off Cannes for the day. Saint-Honorat Island is home to a monastery dating back to AD 410 and has been inhabited by Cistercian monks since the 1800s. The minute I landed, I felt at peace. Visitors had to talk quietly, if at all. The gardens and monastery itself were breathtaking, and as I walked the grounds I just let my emotions take me away. The day was grey and drizzly, so eventually I went inside the monastery and soon found myself alone in one of the rooms. Except I wasn't alone. Jeff was there. It was eerie but comforting at the same time. I was looking through this little window of the monastery and taking photos when I felt his presence. He was very there. He came to say goodbye to me. He said, "You have got to get going. You are young." I wasn't liking him right then. I asked, "What do you mean?" But he didn't say anything else and then he was gone. The room I was in had benches, and as I sat down on one of them I sobbed, great heaving sobs. And then sunlight poured into the room. Where did the sun come from?

When I look at the photo of that window, I know it was a pivotal moment. I believed with all my heart that the only way I was ever going to "move on" was for Jeff to give me that permission. I trusted him when he said I had to get going. I didn't want to be sad forever, but I didn't know how to honour his life while moving on with mine. I didn't think I had the right to be happy when his life had been cut so short. He knew what I needed; he knew that I needed his blessing to live without him.

At one point later in my trip I wanted to go back, back to the island, to the window. I thought that maybe I misunderstood him, or he didn't mean it. In some ways I was so mad at him. Why did he get to decide what was right for me? Maybe if I went back he would talk to me again; maybe he'd keep coming to see and talk to me. But I didn't go back, and it was okay. I did want to build a new life. I didn't want to be alone forever. I had my picture. And I had the memory of his voice in my heart.

People have asked me if I was angry with Jeff and honestly, except for that brief moment in the monastery, I don't think I was. He was working on a movie at the time of his death. The cast and crew had been out celebrating the completion of filming. He knew he shouldn't drive his car, so the director of the film drove it. I remember thinking, "I can't believe you got in that car." And then, at almost the same time, thinking, "Of course you did." It was his car, and even though he knew he shouldn't get in, he did. Jeff was a risk taker. Before we met, he was a professional athlete whose career ended because of an injury. He hung off of buildings as an ironworker. He was a scuba diver and also did underwater welding, a very dangerous job. He rode a motorcycle. That's how he lived his life. When we first got together, he told me that he was probably not going to live a long life because of some of the things that he really loved to do. I thought that was absolute hogwash. "How could you know?" I thought. So was I angry? I don't really remember being angry with Jeff. I felt deep sorrow for not getting to see where life would take him. He was on a path to become an actor, and I knew he would make a career of it. And I was grateful that he taught me to take a few risks of my own (like buying a house at twenty-four, or not having every minute of every day planned to the millisecond!)—something that was not in my DNA.

However, I did direct my anger at the driver of the vehicle. He had been charged in Jeff's death, and the hearing was scheduled for May 16, 1999. I couldn't bring myself to fly to Calgary and face him in court.

Could he possibly understand what he had taken from me? From Jeff's family? In the victim impact statement I wrote for the court I said, "It is nearly twenty months since the car driven by MH claimed my husband's life. Over that time, I have had to learn to live without the man that I loved as much as life itself. Facing MH is something I cannot bear thinking about . . . My life was altered at his hands, and it is unbearable for me to think he is carrying on with his life while mine has been shattered . . ." and on the letter went in that vein for several pages. So yes, there was anger, a lot of anger, but I don't remember ever being angry with Jeff.

When I got back from France it was early May. My boss called me and said, "I'd like you to come back to work." I was scared. I said, "I don't know how to do that. I don't know how I can do that." She said, "I want you to come back into a supervisor position. There will be a little bit of clinical work on a medical day unit, but otherwise it'll be in a supervisory position." I thought about it for a couple of weeks and thought, "I can do that." In hindsight, it was a good decision. I was working with people who had been so supportive all the way along and who continued to support me in my return. Like so many times previously, here was someone again who knew what I needed more than I knew what I needed. And it worked out. I was terrified of doing clinical work, but these children were coming in for day treatments and it was very manageable. I only went back to work part-time. My sleep remained elusive and I found I still needed time to recoup my energy. But going back to work was a very, very good decision. And I know I wouldn't have made that decision on my own. I was lifted up by a caring person and guided toward the future.

When I think about my journey through the loss and grief that followed Jeff's death, I remember how people cared for me. I felt so supported and loved. I had so many friends who knew what to do with me and for me long before I knew what to do with myself. On the flip side, there were also a lot of people who had strong opinions, who wanted to give me advice, lots of advice. They wanted to know where I was going to live because they thought I should move. I didn't even understand that question. I thought, "Why would I live anywhere else? This is my home. What do you mean where am I going to live?" Impossible questions!

And then there came the moment when I could push back against the good intentions. I started to find my own voice and I was able to say to people, "You know what, I'll move when I damn well want to move, and I'll do what I want to do when I'm damn well ready to do it." This was important for me and to me. I had taken small steps back into my life, and pushing back was another step. I don't know how that change came about but there was a definite shift.

I also thought a lot about all those kids and families that I had worked with, and that played a really huge role in my own road back. In the years leading up to Jeff's death, I had worked at BC Children's Hospital long enough (nine years) to have experienced a number of deaths on the adolescent unit. Every one of those youth and families taught me something—mostly about living rather than dying. Working with youth and families also taught me that to survive in my chosen profession, I had to figure out how to create better boundaries, both personal and professional. I was new enough in the profession to not always have the best grasp on these, but if I was going to keep doing this work, I had to be in control of my emotions—finding that emotional strength to do the work. I feel like this all prepared me in some way to better cope, get through, be resilient after Jeff died.

I can't imagine people who don't have a support system going through a loss like I did, or any kind of loss that claims your old life. And you learn who your true supports are. I was so grateful for the people who didn't shy away from talking about Jeff. I was surprised that some of my friends found it difficult to talk about him and, eventually, found it difficult to be around me. I didn't blame people because I'm sure I wasn't always easy to be around. Those who were comfortable talking about death, grief, and loss became even closer friends. I didn't always want to talk about it, but I appreciated those that could just roll with my emotional roller coaster.

One thing I distinctly remember is meeting a woman named Liz. We were having dinner with a mutual friend. She referred to us as "The Merry Widows!" and thought we might enjoy each other's company. Liz had lost her husband a few years after Jeff died. Like me she was young, and when she told me her story, it felt like my own . . . and I was so comforted that there was someone else who had such a similar story. We talked about what happened to us, how we felt, what people did or didn't do that supported us. We had similar experiences with extended family, with antics of our husband's families, and with friends who suddenly disappeared because they didn't know what to say or do. At one point we looked at each other and burst out laughing. "When did widowhood become a contagious disease?" we asked each other. It was a comfort and a relief that someone else "got it," that someone else was riding that crazy emotional roller coaster too.

From time to time I stop and think about who I am today because I lost Jeff, and I realize that I am tough! And I have no regrets. I have no regrets about my marriage with Jeff. I don't wish I had done or said anything differently. I loved him deeply, I felt loved deeply by him, and we were good for each other. Another excerpt from my victim impact statement was "Fortunately, I am now able to remember the love and laughter he brought to my life with fewer tears, and my constant thoughts of him are often accompanied with a smile—I have the comfort of knowing I was loved." I am sure I could have done some things a hundred different ways after he died, but I did the best I could. I remember reading something about temporary suffering, and I firmly believed I would "get through it." Having no regrets was a big part of that.

When I look back on the relationship with my parents, I feel the same way. When they died, I had no regrets. I was a good daughter. And I dealt with my mom and dad's deaths differently because I lost Jeff when I was so young. In many ways, Jeff's death prepared me for future losses. While I wouldn't go so far as to say I was ready for my parents' deaths, I also knew that I would be okay if I didn't have regrets, if I did as much for them as I possibly could, including being with them as much as possible given I lived several hours away. I was loved fiercely by Jeff and by my mom and my dad. Having that love helped carry me through the loss of each of them.

When I think about what I would say to someone who loses a loved one, old clichés come to mind, and they aren't often helpful. "Time heals"—time helps but there will forever be a hole, a missing piece. "You're young, you'll move on"—even if it happens, these are not words a young widow wants to hear. "What doesn't kill you makes you stronger"—again, not helpful. I was strong enough and I wanted Jeff back.

People go through this process in so many different ways. There is no one right way, no magic bullet. Now I try not to ask people what they need, but just anticipate their needs and do things. That is what people did for me: they took charge around me and did things. I couldn't have told them what I needed, but they knew. That's kind of the way I roll now. When my friend Cindy was dying, I would go and get her, take her out if she was able. Or go and do things for her that just needed to be done—like helping her sort through her belongings, purge what she didn't want or need, and organize what was left. Practical. Less questions. More doing.

Grief has no timeline. I tried to stop my grief and it was a disaster. Grief groups can be helpful, but comparing your grief to others like I did wasn't good for me. I try to cut people some slack. It could even be the death of a pet. I have seen people who didn't recover from that. And that's okay. I remember more than a handful of people telling me it was time to move on, to get rid of Jeff's clothes and his things. Lots of opinions! But there were so many memories surrounding me, and I needed to be with those memories. Remember Jeff's clothes that my brother helped me move to my girlfriend's house? They stayed there for many years. I had moved twice before she called me and said, "Do you know these are still here?" I laughed and said yes, and I thought, "I guess it's time." I know people were well-intentioned, but it didn't always help.

I received gift after gift after gift from everyone around me. Not *things*. Gifts of time, of compassion, of love. I am still in awe. As I said earlier, I can't imagine people going through this kind of experience alone, not having support. I had a team around me. I felt like everybody had a corner of a blanket, and when I fell, I just got to bounce back up. People from every chapter of my life were holding a piece of the blanket—my friends from the good old days, my new friends, my hospital friends, my family. I know it wasn't just luck. I guess I chose friends wisely. And you can't choose your family, but mine was pretty awesome. There wasn't just one thing that helped me. It was this package that all came together.

I have been resilient for as long as I can remember. My parents had some turbulent times during my childhood, and I remember clearly asking my mom once how and why she hung in like she did. Her response was direct; it was one of strength and almost defiance. I remember being taken aback and a bit shocked when she told me I didn't understand everything she had gone through for her family. And she was right—it was years later when I was able to see, to understand, and to love her even more for being the glue holding our family together.

I attribute so much of my ability to cope with adverse situations to the depth of friendships I have. I have true lifelong friendships, the longest being fifty-five years, starting with our parents being friends before we were even born. Could resilience also come from where we grew up? I don't know the answer, but I do feel that growing up in a small town and having these deep and lasting friendships helped in some way.

I also studied things in school that helped me move forward. In my Child Life studies we learned so much about ourselves. We stripped that onion. We took courses on resilience, on how to help others, and on how to help ourselves. I learned what self-care looked like and how to do it. I dug deep and felt very raw during those four years of school. And because of that hard work, I became a good reflective practitioner. This practice bolstered my resilience.

When Jeff first died, I did wonder how I was going to carry on. Another excerpt from my victim impact statement said, "The numbness is replaced by the hard reality that Jeff will never walk through our apartment doors. I have felt on numerous occasions that the only way to ease the pain would be to join Jeff," but I go on to say that the love, comfort, and support of friends and family was my saving grace. I learned to trust myself, to be in tune with my feelings. It took time and wasn't always perfect, but I realized I could "feel" whatever I needed to, especially sadness and grief, without worrying that I was going to slip into some deep abyss and never get out. Conversely, when I did have times of happiness and joy after Jeff died, I learned to manage the guilty feelings and trusted those around me to not judge.

And I took the lessons on self-care to heart, doing specific things to care for myself. I remember one Christmas distinctly. I told my mom and dad that I had to work. I told other people I was going up to my mom and dad's. And I stayed home. I just wanted to bury my head that Christmas. I wasn't worried about myself because I knew I would get out of bed in two or three days, but I knew others would worry about me. I played a couple of those games because I needed that time alone. I knew myself well enough to know I could slip into that solitude for a few days, but I wouldn't slip into it for a lifetime.

I never said goodbye to Jeff, not like he did. I was so afraid that if I said goodbye, he wouldn't come to visit me anymore. He did stop visiting right after my trip to France. I was so sad when he said goodbye, but there was also peace. He was right—it was time for me to move forward. I had already opened up to the fact that I wasn't going to waste away. Even to this day, I haven't said a formal goodbye. I didn't, and still don't, need to.

Today is three days before the anniversary of Jeff's death. Twenty-three years. What has struck me about being interviewed for this book is how clear some memories are and how others are so fuzzy or incomplete. Twenty-three years ago I never would have imagined I could forget one single detail of the nightmare I was going through, and yet time does allow some of it to become duller. And that now feels like a blessing.

I don't like being home in the middle of September. I make it a point to be out of town. I've had the luxury some years of the memory of Jeff's death not being the focus of my day. I'm travelling, and so I'm doing something else at the time. That's what I choose. My birthday is four days after the day Jeff died, and they are tied together forever in my mind. I don't like to be home on either day. For many years September 18 could come and go with a gentle nod but not too much attention, but interestingly, in the last five years or so, more memories of him have emerged. My friend Joanne connects with me every year on the 18th. She'll always ask what my day was like, and some years, like the last few, have been more profound than others.

All these years later, some interesting and significant things have popped up for me. I no longer need the ritual of going to Jeff's memorial bench every year to feel close to him. I had a few years where I was an emotional wreck leading up to September 18, but that hasn't been the case recently. And while I can't always recall every detail of our life together, significant memories are imprinted. I can remember his laugh or the sound of his voice when I want to. I still have some things of his that I like to look at. I pulled out a few not that long ago. I have new friends who didn't know I was married before. I was running with one of them yesterday, and after we finished I pulled out some photos and shared them with her. I think she was concerned it would upset me to talk about Jeff or see his photos. In fact, it's quite the opposite. I don't have a lot of occasions anymore to honour the man he was, so it was nice to share a bit about him.

I was so grateful to have such a great job that I could throw myself into, and I wasn't afraid that I would never have another relationship. Of course, that was the other thing people had opinions about—how quickly I would jump into a new relationship. It would seem society has a prescribed "grieving period," but they don't actually tell you how long it is. After two years I was told both gently and emphatically that it was time to move on . . . and also that it was too soon. By then I was stronger, and I had made up my own mind about what I was ready for.

Two years after Jeff died, a dear friend asked me if I would be ready to date again. I didn't know if I was, but I trusted her implicitly. She assured me that the person she was thinking of was kind, smart, and that we had some things in common. I married that man five years after Jeff died. He didn't always have it easy—as he said to me at the beginning of our relationship, "I feel like I'm competing with a ghost." But thankfully, he stuck with me, is understanding, and accepts me for who I am. That includes my life with Jeff and the memories I hold from that time. I wouldn't be happy if it was any other way.

Am I resilient? Yes.

Kim's Reflection

As my interview with Diane ended, I was struck once again by her poise and her thoughtful responses to my questions. I knew her first as a very young woman, excited about the future. I watched with delight as her love for Jeff blossomed, and I stood nearby as she searched for balance after he died.

Two of the themes in the literature on resilience came to mind as I reflected on Diane's story. The first concept was the idea of "facing down reality" that Jim Collins saw in James Stockdale. This is the notion that you must acknowledge what has happened before you can begin to put the pieces back together. The picture will not be the same because that old picture has been smashed, but if you can accept what has happened, you will begin to see glimmers of a new possible life. Frankl's notion regarding the acceptance of the new reality is similar. He believed that each of us must find a way to be realistic about what is "now" and then make a plan to move forward. Diane did that. As much as she wished her life could go back to the way it had been, she knew that was impossible, and she slowly began to look for a new future.

The second theme came from Frankl's work: "life holds a potential meaning under any circumstance even the most miserable ones" (p. xiv). Diane began to find meaning in her new life. She walked through the grief, that desolate time, and began to embrace a life that held meaning for her. She stopped asking "why me" because there was no answer to that question. Instead, she lifted her head up. She didn't know how to move forward; she just knew she had to because Jeff wouldn't expect anything else. Work gave her the meaning she needed, and once she gave it a chance, the rest of her new life began to fall into place. The saying "Just keep putting one foot in front of the other" can sound trite, but that is what Diane did, and she was surrounded by friends who would catch her on the days when instead of going forward she felt like she was frozen in one spot. But the next moment or hour or day she would carry on, and the new meaning she found in life grew in different ways.

The seed of inner strength that started to grow when Diane was a little girl flourished in the most demanding of times. She instinctively reached out for a way to reorient herself to living. Her sadness didn't vanish — but her desire to live fully, to not be a victim, rekindled a tiny flame, and her resilience fanned that flame, making it brighter, stronger, carrying her toward the next phase in her life. I can feel Jeff smiling.

CHAPTER TWO: DODIE

Kim's Story

I MET DODIE ON OCTOBER 31, 1988—*Halloween. Halloween is a big deal in a children's hospital, and BC Children's Hospital, where we both worked, was no exception. Staff were expected to arrive in costume and be ready to parade around the wards in costume all day! I was dressed as Swee'Pea, a character from Popeye, and Dodie was dressed as a construction worker, with a costume that included a real saw and hammer. (I think her house was going through a renovation at the time, so she borrowed the necessary equipment.) Our friendship developed steadily from there. We had the same boss, and that made for lots of gossipy conversations. We laughed a lot! We loved our jobs, both believing that what we did was important. But life changed for both of us—my husband was offered a job in Hong Kong and we moved our family to the other side of the world. Shortly after that, Dodie's husband had an opportunity to work in Australia for a year, so she left her job at the hospital and headed off on a new adventure. But even though we went off on these new journeys, our friendship remained intact. Over the next ten years we continued to be champions for each other. We would get together for lunch or dinner, catch up on each other's life, and talk about whatever was on our minds. The conversations swung from topic to topic like a pendulum—family, work, politics. Never dull and always filled with laughter.*

We had dinner together shortly before the mammogram that changed everything. My life continued along its bumpy way, but Dodie's—well, her life took an unexpected turn. Cancer came calling.

Over the next days and weeks I stayed in touch with Marty, Dodie's husband. I learned as much as I could about her diagnosis and tried to help wherever possible, keeping her company at some of her hours-long chemo sessions. But at the end of the day, I felt helpless. As the months passed, I watched Dodie struggle. Then, slowly, her response to her cancer changed. She became calmer, more at ease with her new reality. Her inner strength began to emerge in ways that surprised her. But it didn't surprise me. From the day I met Dodie, I could see a deep resilience in her. She radiated a grit that allowed her to challenge many of life's expectations, and she did it with grace and humour.

Dodie's strength has been challenged over and over in the last twenty years as cancer invaded other parts of her body, but she continues to stand strong. She is a wife, a mother, a grandmother, a volunteer. Her life's journey included time as an accomplished journalist, a musician, and an equestrian. And she is a woman with cancer. She lives side by side with this disease, but it doesn't rule who she is. She isn't fighting cancer—she is fighting to live fully. That, for her, is what it means to be resilient.

Dodie's Story

It was April 2, 2001, a warm spring day. My husband, Marty, was in Whistler, skiing. I had gone for dinner the night before with a friend. I went for a run that morning and planned to go to a fitness class later in the day. I was really into being fit and thought that my health was excellent.

I went to my 1 p.m. mammogram appointment at a radiology clinic on the east side of Vancouver. My mammograms were not done through a regular screening clinic because I had "dense breasts," a common condition now recognized as a risk factor for breast cancer. I'd been referred by my long-time family doctor. I had no particular expectations, no big concerns. When the radiology tech was finished taking her pictures, she had the radiologist come in and feel my left breast. I remember thinking, "This can't be good." The doctor asked that additional images be taken. I assume he reviewed them right away because he came back in and said,

"Come back tomorrow for a biopsy." There was no explanation, but I put two and two together and interpreted that he suspected cancer.

I drove home. Marty wasn't back yet from Whistler, but as soon as I saw his car drive up, I walked out to greet him, leaving the front door wide open. Our son David, nineteen, had just finished his first year of university and was at home. He had no idea where I had gone nor why I left the door open—not my usual practice. I got into Marty's car and said, "I think I have breast cancer." We drove down to the beach and talked. I don't remember the exact conversation, but I suppose we promised to support each other, and we decided not to tell David and our daughter Jenny, twenty-one, the bad news until it was confirmed.

Marty came with me the next day when I went for the biopsy, a painful procedure involving repeated needle thrusts into my breast to remove bits of tissue for analysis. The radiologist—the same one I'd seen the day before—didn't explain much to us but congratulated the technician on the good job she was doing. After it was finished, the radiologist said, "You'd better get yourself a good surgeon. You're going to need it." In that moment I was scared but I was also angry. I knew he had to give me the bad news but was there no gentler way? As we parted, my final thought was, "So much for compassion!"

Things moved very quickly after the biopsy. The first thing I had to do was find a surgeon. I called my family doctor, who happened to be out of town, but her receptionist recommended a surgeon and I made an appointment. It all happened so fast! The mammogram was on a Monday, the biopsy was on a Tuesday, and by Friday I was seeing a surgeon. I don't know if that would happen today, but this was nearly twenty years ago.

The surgeon was a lovely, warm woman who seemed to understand that a cancer diagnosis would be devastating. She said something like, "It looks localized and relatively small. We can just do a lumpectomy"— a smaller procedure than a mastectomy, which is removal of the whole breast. She set a surgery date and sent me for some routine pre-op blood work.

The next day she called me and said, "I'm sorry, but we can't do the surgery. Your cancer is metastatic. I can tell from the blood work that it has already spread." The lab results showed that my liver enzymes were elevated, affecting liver function. She said, "I want you to go see an oncologist." I knew the name Karen Gelmon from a friend so I asked, "Can you refer me to Dr. Gelmon?"

Within two days I was in Karen Gelmon's office at the BC Cancer Agency Vancouver Centre. I liked her immediately. She was direct and already seemed knowledgeable about my case. She had reviewed all the test results before my appointment. She said, "We can't cure your disease, but we can manage it—for a while." I started chemo that Thursday, just before the Easter long weekend, and spent the next four days throwing up. I was so new to this cancer thing that I didn't know there were drugs that could help with nausea or that I could have called the cancer clinic for advice; there's a doctor on call twenty-four hours a day.

On the Tuesday after the long weekend, Marty called Dr. Gelmon, who told him to bring me to the clinic where they would give me fluids to re-hydrate. She said, "I'm sorry. This won't happen again because we're going to give you some drugs next time." For several more months I was on this traditional chemo, the kind that causes your hair to fall out and makes you vomit, but the anti-nausea drugs did help make the treatments more tolerable.

There's no doubt that I was in shock. In the years leading up to my diagnosis, life was good. After leaving Children's Hospital I had started a consulting business, and it was going very well. But now my life fell apart. Everything crashed.

My whole family was in shock. Our daughter, Jenny, had just been accepted to the University of Toronto master of social work program. She said, "I don't want to go. I want to stay here and help you." I said, "No. No, I want you to go." And followed up with all those motherly things like "I don't want my health to interfere with your life." She did move to Toronto for the first year of the two-year program, then decided to come back home, saying, "Mom, it's not your decision anymore." She, David, Marty, and I knew that metastatic cancer was at that time usually a death sentence. But as a family we came together. In early July they joined my friends in a surprise party for my fifty-second birthday. We all thought it would probably be my last.

At the end of July, four months after my diagnosis, Karen said, "I'm going to take you off this chemo. It isn't working. There's a new treatment that I want you to try."

I said, "I don't want to do it. I've had enough chemo. I'm tired of being sick all the time. I've come to terms with this." I had reached the conclusion that if I had to go on being so sick and debilitated, with no hope of a cure, I didn't want to live any longer. I was serious about it. My mother used to say to me "'quality versus quantity" because I'm short. And I thought, "Quality versus quantity."

Karen called Marty and said, "She would be foolish not to try this. This could be *the* designer drug for your wife." I don't know how, but she convinced me, and I started the new regime.

The drug was called Herceptin, one of the first in a new class of "magic bullet" drugs that attack a cancer cell but don't damage healthy cells. It doesn't make you sick and your hair doesn't fall out. It was no longer experimental, but it wasn't for everyone. It's only effective for women with breast cancer who have a very specific protein, called human epidermal growth factor receptor 2 (HER2), in their system. If you didn't have that protein, getting this very expensive drug would be like drinking Kool-Aid—it wouldn't help you at all. But for the 20 to 30 percent of breast cancer patients who have the protein, it can be magic. Analysis of my tumour showed that it was 100 percent positive for this protein. HER2+ breast cancer is a particularly aggressive variety that tends to affect younger women.

Karen prescribed an IV infusion of Herceptin at the cancer clinic every three weeks with the hope that it would be magic for me too. But it didn't work immediately.

I had an ultrasound scan on September 11, 2001 (9/11, when most of the world was watching in horror the news from the World Trade Center). That night my family doctor, also a long-time friend, came to our house with a piece of paper in her hand. She said, "The scan report shows that you have innumerable tumours throughout your liver." Marty and I were again thrown into shock. We sat with Ellen, my doctor, for over an hour doing end-of-life planning and grappling with questions like "How long do I have? How do I want to die? At home? In hospital? In a hospice?" For whatever reason, the magic drug had not worked for me.

Once more I was ready to call it quits. (This was, of course, years before the legalization of MAiD, Medical Assistance in Dying.) But again, Karen was persuasive and talked me into giving Herceptin another couple of months. Weeks later my liver started to improve. The scans showed fewer tumours. I started to feel better. My hair started to grow back. Life returned to something like normal.

Fast-forward two decades. I've had several recurrences. The cancer has come back in my brain, (requiring surgery to remove a frontal-lobe tumour), my spine, my liver, and my ribs, treated with various forms of IV chemo, radiation, and oral drugs. After a recurrence at the original site eight years after my initial diagnosis, my left breast was removed with a mastectomy. April 2, 2021, marked twenty years since my diagnosis. I'm still going to the cancer clinic for a monthly treatment with Herceptin and a similar drug, Pertuzumab, adding up to a total of about four hundred chemo treatments. And yet here I am.

I've had help along the way. In 2001, personal medical history—doctors' comments, test reports—was not available to patients like it is today under freedom of information laws. We patients were not supposed to see our medical charts, but I would sneak mine off the nurse's desk when I went for chemo. I read that the first time Karen Gelmon met me, she wrote in the chart something like, "This is a very practical woman, and the hardest thing is going to be giving up her sense of control of her life." And I thought, "Bingo. That's me!" I was not coping well, crying through every appointment. I was just such a mess. After a few months of this, Karen said, "You need to talk to someone. Go see Janie Brown."

Janie Brown studied nursing in her native Scotland before moving to Canada, where she worked as an oncology nurse. She began to feel that many patients were receiving excellent medical care, but their emotional and spiritual needs were not always being met. She decided to change that. At that point, the worst thing that had happened to me so far in my cancer journey was that the cancer had metastasized to my liver, a vital organ. She asked me to lie down on her couch and put her hand on my abdomen, saying, "If you die from cancer in your liver, you won't be in pain. You'll just get sleepy over a period of days. We can control any discomfort very well with medication." She helped me to not be afraid of dying.

Our sessions initially were about dying, getting used to the likelihood that I was near the end of my life and learning to manage my complicated feelings about that. Then we moved on to exploring unresolved issues so that when I died, I would have no big regrets. She helped me think through many things, like my connections with parents and other relatives, and my anger and disappointment about the cancer's damage to my physical abilities, career, and family. My relationship with Janie became very deep and meaningful to me. She continues to have that impact on the many people she helps through her counselling practice and through the activities of the Callanish Society, the organization she created to support people with cancer and their families. Though I no longer see her often in person, I try to stay connected. She's a wise, gifted, loving woman.

How am I now? I don't know. Usually I can stay positive, grateful that I moved decades ago from the United States to Canada, where I've gotten superb care under our public health system. Sometimes I feel sad, angry, and regretful about the fact that my life has changed so much. I had to let go of a lot of things when I was diagnosed, including my career. There are still times when I resent that I had to give that up. When I was younger, I considered myself a feminist, and working was a big part of my self-image, my identity. After my diagnosis, work could no longer be a priority.

Usually I can flip back and feel thankful that I have now lived past my seventy-first birthday, especially when I remember that my initial prognosis at fifty-one was twelve to eighteen months. I know so many people who have not made it. When I'm sitting in the chemo chair, I can almost tell what kind of cancer people have by the drug they are getting. I know if they're on an experimental trial drug, they probably have no other options. It's unlikely that they're going to be alive in twenty years. They may not even be there the next month. So I wouldn't say it's effortless, but I do try to stay in a space of gratitude. I think of these twenty years as bonus "Air Miles." And I try to be a productive member of society, to somehow pay back for what I have received. I volunteer at a local museum, in my Jewish community, and I help friends who are dealing with mental or physical health problems.

I'm certainly not a trained counsellor, but I think I've learned enough through my own experience to be helpful. If asked by someone just diagnosed with a serious disease or facing a major life crisis, I might suggest, "Decide what *you* want—don't be influenced by what somebody else wants you to do. You can listen to what they say, but the final decision is yours. Either with a counsellor or just by finding some quiet time for yourself, figure out what's right for you. That will help you make those difficult decisions." We don't have control over everything (whether it's about going ahead with another treatment option, starting or leaving a job or relationship, moving, or having another child), but we do have choices, decisions that are ours to make. The minute I was diagnosed with cancer I began to lose personal power in my life. Suddenly I was dependent on the opinion of doctors, my normal routine being replaced by medical appointments, tests, and treatments. I've learned that a sense of loss of power or control is common for people diagnosed with cancer, and I often share my experience with others, hoping it will help them.

The lesson I was learning in the time just after my diagnosis was about control. We think we control our lives to a great extent, or at least I did. I was busy with my career and my family, booking trips and events months in advance. I couldn't do that anymore, because I never knew how I was going to feel. I realized that I couldn't control everything. I'm not enough of a believer to think that there's a superior being up in the sky who's organizing everything that happens, but, however it works, I know that we humans are not in control. I'm reminded of this again with the impact of COVID-19. There is so much uncertainty in the world right now with the ongoing pandemic, and uncertainty isn't something most of us are used to or feel comfortable with. People are struggling everywhere to figure out how to live differently day to day. Planning ahead holds a new meaning. Maybe we can see a few days ahead but not months and certainly not years. I'd already gotten used to planning very few things in advance. Cancer has helped me learn to accept uncertainty.

I was trained as a journalist, and when I was diagnosed I started reading everything I could find about cancer. I began to notice commercial ventures supporting things like "April is Breast Cancer Month. If you buy this kind of laundry detergent or that kind of cereal, two cents of every million dollars of profit will go to breast cancer research." It seemed like a scam! I also became very sensitive to the military language often used about cancer. You see it all the time in obituaries: *She lost her fight with cancer . . . He died after a long battle with cancer . . .* The language implies that those with cancer are soldiers in a war, and I don't like that idea. Learning to live with cancer makes a lot more sense. Fighting all the time takes so much energy; learning to live with a disease that was now, after all, a part of me, helped me to be more at ease with my new life.

From the start it was still possible to find joy. Riding horses was one way I could feel joyful despite my health problems. I had wanted to ride horses since I was a child forced to take piano lessons! When I was in my forties, my time was a little more my own, so I started taking English riding lessons on an old mare named Goldie. I learned to bring her in from her paddock, brush her, clean her feet, wrap her legs, and saddle her. I even tried a bit of jumping and wonder now how I managed not to fall off and break my neck.

I was too sick to ride during the early days, but after the first few months of treatment I called Robyn, my trainer, and went back to weekly lessons on Goldie. I kept riding for several more years. Karen Gelmon first said, "It's bad for your spine but good for your soul." After a while that switched to her saying, "It's good for your soul, but it's really bad for your spine." I miss riding terribly but appreciate that it helped me fulfill a childhood dream. I value the healing non-verbal communication I had with Goldie and with the other animals in my life, my much-loved cats Oscar and Lucy. Now, having unexpectedly survived long enough to have four grandchildren, I find joy knowing that I will in some way live on through them.

From the beginning a sense of humour helped me. A few things happened in the early days that made me laugh. There is a term I learned— "casserole lady." Marty was a good-looking guy (still is). He was only fifty-five and not yet retired. Single women looking for a guy like that and anticipating my imminent demise would bring over a casserole. For some reason I found that funny. Guess I've fooled them! What makes me laugh now? Silly jokes from my grandkids, like "Why won't the clam share his snack? Because he's a little shellfish." Or "What kind of shoes does a banana wear? Slippers."

During that time right after my diagnosis, I found out who my real friends were. For some people it was like: "Well, Dodie eats kale and brown rice, she works out, lives a healthy life. If *she* can get cancer, anybody can get it—*I* could get it!" That was too scary for some, and they weren't comfortable being with me. I was particularly surprised by one friend who just dropped out of my life. I realized over time that it was her own fear that kept her away, and I feel sorry for her that she was unable to learn from my experience. Other people, even those I didn't know that well, surprised me with their willingness to talk, drive me to appointments, and help in whatever way they could.

Being Jewish has been a support for me. My family is not deeply religious, but I have a great appreciation for the values of Judaism. It deals very well with death and mourning, placing loss in the context of the cycle of life, with new babies growing into children and adults, eventually aging and dying, leaving room for a new generation. In customs and rituals, there's always a recognition that each of us is on earth for a limited time, and that we must learn to make the most of that. A basic principle of being Jewish is "Tikkun olam," a Hebrew expression that means "Repair of the world." As Jews, we are commanded to live in a way that leaves the world a bit better than when we came into it. I hope that I will leave the world a bit better than when I arrived.

Despite all the stress of ongoing treatment and recurrences, I don't think I have changed too much over the years. I think that people have a core essence of *being*. You, me, everyone. A truly religious person might call it a soul. My life has certainly changed. I haven't been able to do the work I used to do or the activities I used to enjoy. But I don't feel I've become a totally different person.

I realized I was stronger than I thought I was. If you had told me a couple of years before I got sick what life was soon going to be like, I would have said, "No, I can't do it." And I have had moments of thinking that I couldn't do it, I didn't want to do it anymore. But here I am, still in the game.

I believe I inherited strength—resilience—from my father. He left his native Germany at the age of twenty-eight because the Nazis wouldn't let him, as a Jew, practise medicine after he'd finished medical school. He escaped Hitler by fleeing to the United States, leaving his parents, friends, and other family members behind. He never saw his parents, my grandparents, again. They were murdered in the concentration camps. My father died in 1993 at eighty-four, after serving as a respected country doctor for fifty-two years in a town of 6,200 people, the town where I was born and raised. I was glad that he didn't have to watch me deal with cancer. I would not have wanted him to endure further pain and loss after losing almost everything once already.

I've been trying for about fifteen years to put together the story of my father and my family history. I have documents, photos, letters, and artifacts from his life before and after he arrived in America, about his efforts to get back property, artwork, and other possessions stolen from his family by the Nazis. He became an American citizen as soon as he was eligible and joined the US Army. Because he could speak German, he got sent right back to Germany, where he was assigned to treat German soldiers in prisoner-of-war camps. I wonder now, "How did he feel about that?" He didn't talk much about any of this—the disruption in his life, the move to a different country, the loss of his parents, and so much more. I wish I had him back. I have so many questions that will remain unanswered.

At this time, it's one of my few regrets that I haven't finished this project. There is so much material! I was getting somewhere until COVID-19 hit, and I lost my focus. But it's always on my mind. I don't want to die, from cancer, COVID-19, or anything else, before I finish this work.

I want my children and grandchildren to know that they come from a family that has been resilient in the face of personal challenges and sometimes unthinkable trauma. I hope that knowing this story will help them deal resiliently with whatever difficulties they face in their own lives. I hope it will tell them, even after I'm no longer here, "You can do it! You're stronger than you think!"

Toda Raba

(Thank you, very much)

Kim's Reflection

When I asked Dodie to be part of my project she was, for a moment, perplexed. She hadn't given much thought to the idea of resilience and didn't see herself as a resilient person. She resisted being called resilient at first. I think she thought the term was too over-used, too kitschy. But when I substituted other descriptors like strong, feisty, spirited *— she began to accept that maybe she was resilient. As we moved through the interview, I could see her putting the various pieces of her life under a light and examining them, looking at each situation differently. By nature she is a curious person and doesn't accept much at face value. My questions made her think about her life from a new perspective.*

I asked Dodie where she thought her grit came from and she began to talk about her father. She realized that his spirit lived in her, something she hadn't thought a lot about before. She also talked about her deep connection to her Jewish faith and the strength she drew from that heritage. She faced adversity and not only survived but actually thrived when she wasn't sure she could or would. She chose to live a full and contented life.

Like James Stockdale, Dodie looks at the world through brutally honest eyes. Once she recovered from the shock of her initial diagnosis and the boundaries cancer created around her future, Dodie took a long, hard look at her life. She didn't kid herself; things were grim. She looked at her predicament and thought, "Now what?" Then she did what resilient people do. Like Frankl, Stockdale, and the other people you will read about, Dodie figured out ways to create new meaning for herself and her family. She didn't withdraw from her life; she just needed to define a different path that would still carry her forward. Cancer slowed her down, but it didn't stop her from living.

Both Frankl and Stockdale said that finding meaning in life is made easier when you have a strong value system. Values help us decide where to put our resources, whatever those resources might be. The doctors initially told Dodie she had only twelve to eighteen months to live, so she had to decide how to use the most precious resource she had: time. While she was working out how to use the time she had left, she was guided by one of her important values: integrity. That value carried her through many difficult choices.

In Harold Kushner's book Living a Life That Matters, *Chapter Five is called "Shalom: The Quest for Integrity." His words remind me of Dodie. She has lived her whole life with integrity, and when she spoke of her father, I understood where Dodie learned that value. He lived a life guided by integrity, and it was one of the things Dodie respected about him. Kushner's chapter focuses on who we will be not just in good times but in difficult times. He says, "There is a consistency to [her], that [she] will be the same person tomorrow that [she] is today and will apply the same value system to one question that [she] does to all questions" (p. 88). I thought, "Ah—that is Dodie! She will apply the same values tomorrow that she did yesterday." From the first day of her new chaotic life with cancer, Dodie lived as she had before. She used her deeply held values as the compass for how to go forward. Face your reality, make meaning of the new order and do so with the guidance of your values. By doing this, you will live life fully, honestly.*

Kushner says that to wish someone shalom means "to wish him or her the blessing of wholeness and integrity" (p. 89). Tenacious, determined, irreverent, and whole, Dodie continues to live her best life. And so I say to her, shalom, Dodie!

CHAPTER THREE: BINDY

Kim's Story

I ENTERED THE CHILD LIFE *office at BC Children's Hospital on August 4, 1988. It was my first day as a Child Life specialist,4 and I was terrified. The room was filled with people chatting, busy preparing for the day. I was greeted by a vivacious blond woman with a huge smile and a big "Hello!" She was so gracious as she showed me around the cramped space, talking a mile a minute about where I could put my bag, where supplies were, and, most importantly, what time we all would go for coffee! That was Bindy.*

I watched Bindy very carefully and learned from her every day. She was so passionate about the importance of the Child Life program and our impact on the well-being of sick children and their families. Whenever I could, I followed her around the wards to see how she interacted with families and kids. I don't think she knew that! I wanted to learn from her because she was such a natural. Bindy knew and modelled the tenets of the program, and I wanted to be like her.

Little did I know that inside this energetic and cheerful woman lived a profound and deep sorrow. I didn't learn until a few weeks later that Bindy's

---

4   Child Life specialists are trained to help children, youth, and families cope with stressors related to illness, hospitalization, trauma, and loss. They are a critical part of the medical team.

daughter, Laura, had died just two years earlier. Then I understood the ease she had with kids and families. She had been in their place; she understood their grief in a way that I didn't. So I kept watching and learning. Our friendship grew slowly, quietly, and has remained strong for over thirty years. She still has that huge smile and gracious nature. And Laura—well, she is right there too. This is Bindy's story—a story of loss, survival, and triumph.

Bindy's Story

My daughter, Laura, was diagnosed with cancer at the very end of October in 1985. She was four years old. During the summer I had taken her to our family doctor because I felt there was something wrong with her. I said, "She's not well, just not herself." Laura wasn't a crybaby—she was a "get things done" kind of kid, on the go all the time, and yet there were these periods of time during the summer when she just didn't feel well. I wasn't concerned at that point about her belly. I guess I thought she was a child with a chubby tummy, and it didn't look abnormal when I first took her to the doctor. But the day our family doctor referred her to a pediatrician, I was really concerned about the way her belly looked. It wasn't just chubby anymore; it was becoming distended. The pediatrician made arrangements for an ultrasound, and then we were admitted to the pediatric unit.

After we were admitted, I remember the resident coming up to the unit. He sat down beside me. He explained to me that they had found something that "looked like a cyst or something" on the ultrasound. Immediately I realized he was trying to soften the blow, that they had found something much more than a cyst. I thought, "Cysts are small, this isn't small." He didn't use the word *tumour*. But I knew it was a tumour. And there was Laura, sitting right beside me, playing with the toys the nurses had brought her. It felt completely unreal.

Laura had surgery the following week. The resident came to see me after surgery. He said they did remove a tumour, but at that point they had no idea what kind of tumour it was. And he waited until the message sank in. I was horrified. I kept saying, "No, not her. No, not her. It can't be. It can't be true." It was an immediate response because I just couldn't take it all in. I wanted to push it away, I didn't want it to be real. The resident was a very gentle man. He sat with me for some time, to comfort me. And he stayed until my parents came.

The tumour weighed about two and a half pounds. Laura was just a little four-year-old and she wasn't a big kid, so two and a half pounds was a lot. She looked pretty thin after that surgery. Kids start to lose their baby fat and stretch out when they turn four years old, so I thought maybe that was why she was looking so thin. But that wasn't it, that wasn't what was happening.

The week after she'd had her surgery, I started having nightmares that really disturbed my sleep. If I fell asleep, I dreamed horrible things. There was no time, night or day, when I was free from this tumour that had no name. I was physically and mentally exhausted all the time, but I had to be positive and normal around Laura. I could never cry, I could never give in to the exhaustion. I would get into the shower when she napped and cry and cry so the tears would wash away. I was a mess. I started grieving the week Laura was diagnosed, right then and there in October.

I talked to my family doctor in that first week after the surgery. At that time nobody had a firm grasp on the diagnosis. About six weeks later he told me that Laura had a Sertoli and Leydig cell tumour, and he said, "Wow, this is a really unusual diagnosis. We know very little about this kind of tumour. There are only seventeen known cases in the literature. That's all that's ever been recorded, and those cases were not children."

The oncologist never told me more than the name of the suspected tumour and that they would treat it like a rhabdomyosarcoma, a more common form of cancer. At the time I accepted the explanation because I knew so little. Once I learned how rare Laura's tumour was, I realized they had no idea how to treat it and were making a best guess. I trusted the doctor less and less as time went on. I asked for information about the treatment protocols several times and never received any answers. I asked the chemo nurses, but they seemed hesitant to go into any "teaching." They said they would ask the doctor to speak to me but that never happened. I began to think that they had no idea if the treatment would work. It was an entirely new diagnosis for them; they were just guessing. I felt information was being withheld, which contributed to a lack of trust I was feeling. None of this was at all helpful to my well-being.

Laura went through several rounds of chemo through the winter and into the spring. Then she had another surgery, removing more tumours. The staff tried to be optimistic after the second surgery. For the second round of chemotherapy, different drugs were prescribed. I asked how that decision was made. If these drugs were so effective, why didn't they try them the first time around? The staff tried to support me by saying that this protocol would be better, more effective. But I knew. I knew she was going to die.

The rationale for the second round of chemo was weak. Nobody convinced me that it was going to be effective. The staff tried really hard to help Laura cope because she was getting wise to how things worked in the hospital. She knew a lot of it was going to be painful and make her sick. The chemo was devastating for her. And it was devastating to me because I knew she was suffering; she couldn't explain the way she felt. She had the words—she could tell you what medications she was taking—but she didn't understand what they did. She would say to people, "I have a tumour in my tummy." It made her sound like she was older than she was and had more understanding, but it was her only way of expressing why she felt so sick. She hated the smell of her skin from the chemo. She insisted on having a Tinkerbell perfume-soaked cotton ball in her hand, and she would hold it to her nose. Panic set in if the cotton ball got lost.

Laura was always trying to gain control. The nurses would let her take the syringe and give herself the medications because they knew she needed control over something in her life. Anything anyone could do that gave her that sense of independence was so important. She wanted to play but she was too weak. She no longer had the life of a child. It was fading away from her and she tried desperately to have some control over it. She insisted on having her doll, Lindsay, with her. She told me what books to read and what songs to sing. She loved music and she loved to sing, even when she was sick. We would sing songs together all the time, and I used her love of music to help her get through some of the difficult times. Because she could no longer run or ride her bike or stand on her head, all the physical things she loved to do, she started painting and copying words from get-well cards onto paper. Doing these quiet, fine motor things made her seem like another child, not the noisy, boisterous, and bossy child we knew. I remember her riding her two-wheeled bike around the co-op complex, shouting, "I am four in September!" Another time, before she was ill, I had taken her to the swimming pool and the first thing she did was climb up the stairs and slide face-first down the slide into the water. She was fearless. She loved life. But that life was slipping away.

She was at Victoria General for the last couple of months of chemo. The physiotherapist would try to get Laura up and doing things after her treatments, but often she didn't want to—Laura could be very obstinate. So I brought in her little Fisher-Price tape recorder and tapes that she liked. I made a tape of us singing songs (I still have it.) She adored the bagpipes, so I would put a tape of bagpipes on, and she would march around the ward to the music. That was her physio! She did it her way. Another favourite song was Fred Penner's "Rollerskating." One day she wore her roller skates from the car across the parking lot and down the hallway of the hospital. She wanted to arrive on her roller skates. She was always struggling, fighting, to be herself. But she was getting weaker and weaker and terribly thin. Part of her was already gone by March 1986.

There was always so much potential in that child. She was interested in so many things and paid attention to everything. A month before she died, she kept saying to me, "Mom, did you register me for French immersion? Did you register me for kindergarten?" She was on my case, making sure I hadn't forgotten. I couldn't say, "You know, honey, you're never going to go to kindergarten." I would say, "I know you really want to go to kindergarten, don't you?" It was heartbreaking. She wanted to learn how to play the violin, the bagpipes—so many things. She was too weak for any of those wishes to come true.

My biggest worry besides Laura was my son, Colin. He was seven and a half years old when Laura was diagnosed. I explained that she had a tumour in her tummy that was making her very sick. I told him that the doctors were trying everything to make her better. I am lucky that he was what you would call an "easy" child. He was always comfortable with new people; he was happy when friends had to look after him. He was just an easygoing little guy. I was a single parent and all I could think about was how was I going to take care of him as well as Laura? But people came, people helped. Family, friends—they just came, and they looked after Colin.

I kept thinking that he was missing out on so much. For almost eight months he had very little time with me. We weren't having all the normal routines of family life. My dear friend and neighbour, Margie, often came over on school mornings and stayed with Laura (Laura loved her!) while I drove Colin to school. At least we had that time in the car together, when we could chat and he didn't have to defer to Laura's needs. I wanted him to know, needed him to know, that I loved him to pieces even though he got so little attention from me. He was a very sweet little boy. I worried about what was going on inside of him all the time, how he was coping with all that was going on around him. Thankfully, we talked openly about Laura, right from the beginning. One day he told me he felt bad because he had punched her in the tummy and made her sick. Imagine if he hadn't been able to say that! I told him that all kids punch their brothers and sisters, and that never makes them have cancer—her illness was definitely not his fault.

I was fortunate to have such a great group of friends. I was living in a little housing co-op, and there were probably twenty kids living there. Everybody knew everybody and we cared for each other as if we were one big family. I was working full-time at the University of Victoria's daycare centre, and I was also going to university part-time in the Child and Youth Care program to become a Child Life specialist. So I was surrounded by people who loved children. And they all loved Colin. I met my friend Deborah working at the daycare, and even though I'd only known her for a couple of years, she helped me so much with Colin. She would pick him up from after-school daycare and bring him home to me or take him to her place, make dinner for him, and bring him home later. Others did those kinds of things too. Even my boss Lucille, who was the program director, picked Colin up from school. She said he was so good. He said, "Hi, Lucille!" got into the car, and away they went. I could always count on my friends.

I knew that he was taken care of each day, but I worried about him in the long run. Laura was dying. He was going to be on his own, no sister. How would he handle that? Would he understand? I worried that he would be traumatized by what was happening to Laura. And of course he was—we both were. But the good thing was we always talked. Even through his teen years, after hanging out with his friends or talking on the phone, he would come into my room at night while I was reading and lie across the end of the bed. We would just talk. It was a habit we got into, and it stayed like that throughout his teens. He had his teenage troubles and gave me some sleepless nights, but at heart he was a good person just trying to find his way in the world. He had a very calm nature; he was a watcher and an observer. And he took the many changes happening in his life in stride. As he got older and life got more complicated, he had his struggles. He has often been hard on himself. He was a late bloomer with a tender heart. He has grown to be a fine man. He is hard-working, loving, kind, funny, and artistic with a huge social circle of great friends. He is happy and that is all we ever want for our children. He and I share lots of "Laura" memories and laugh, and we will always do that. We both wonder who she would be now, and how life would be with her here, if she had lived.

The eight months that Laura was sick was an exhausting period of time. So little sleep—never enough. Laura was not a good sleeper before she got sick, and it only got worse once she started chemo. She would be in the hospital for five days at a time and be sick the whole time. Then we'd go home and she'd be sick for another two weeks. We'd have one week where she was feeling better and not vomiting all the time. We would sleep that week. And then start all over again. I still sleep poorly. I think that pattern was set when Laura was sick. Never, never enough sleep.

Laura died at Victoria General in June 1986, under the care of Victoria Hospice. She always had the same room when she was admitted, and she called it "my room." She walked straight in there whenever we arrived. She knew the staff and they had a pretty good handle on her too. It was a place she was comfortable, and I needed the support of the staff. I could never have managed at home.

The staff were amazing in the final days. They worked closely with Jim Wilde, the hospice doctor who took over Laura's care when she was admitted for the last time. He would come in to see her regularly, talk to her about what she was doing. Sometimes she would answer, sometimes not—she tolerated him! But he was a wonderful help to me. He would talk to me about how best to care for her and what to expect as dying progressed. He worked with the staff to create a plan that would make Laura as comfortable as possible. She didn't want an IV, so he and the pharmacist made morphine suppositories that she could insert herself. It became more and more difficult as the days passed, and I was so grateful that the team made all those accommodations to help her. Laura's independent nature prevailed right to the end. Even the day she died, she insisted on getting up and going to the bathroom. I had to lift her onto the toilet, and when I tried to steady her so she wouldn't fall, she held on to the bar and said, "I can do it myself." She was her true self right until the end of her life.

I was devastated when Laura died. I knew it was coming but that didn't make it easier. And I was exhausted. I had wanted to spend every minute of the day with her for as many days as we had, and that meant giving up sleep. I had wanted to make her life the best it could possibly be under the circumstances, and that meant being awake at any time to respond to whatever she needed for comfort. And to make sure her pain was under control. I had wanted to do all the things she loved: singing songs, reading stories, making sure my parents could be with her at any time. I still remember the feeling of her head tucked in the crook of my neck when she snuggled on my lap, and the feeling of her little thin hand in mine. It was hard to recall a time when those hands were chubby. Maybe it was because she moved so fast and it was hard to catch her, to hold her close. Those last days were awful and wonderful.

We had a quiet memorial for Laura with friends and family. At first Colin decided that he didn't want to come. I said that was okay and I arranged for him to stay with someone. But then he changed his mind, and I remember how he held my hand throughout. Before we left home, I explained that lots of the grownups would cry, including me, and I remember telling him that Uncle Steve (who wasn't really an uncle but a dear friend) and "Yo" (as Colin called Steve's wife, Cecilia) would cry too. I think I just wanted to make it really real, so he would not be shocked when it happened.

We also had a gathering for Laura's daycare friends, our neighbours, and our friends' children. We all walked from the co-op down along a stream in a nearby park, where the kids liked to play. We sat together in the field and I read them some of Laura's favourite stories, including *Frog and Toad*. My friend Pat played her guitar and sang all Laura's favourite songs, including "Morningtown Ride." There was something so calming in that lullaby.

I cried every day after she died, and I cried every day for I don't know how many years. I cried on the way to work, I cried on the way home from work. I couldn't stop the tears; they just flowed. The grief is there. You don't get over it. There's no getting over it. You get through it, absorb it. It becomes a part of who you are. Because of my grief I probably wasn't as attentive to Colin as I should have been. Over the years I avoided getting into the teenager arguments. He did stupid teenage things and I was probably too relaxed, but it was too hard to do anything else. In the first few years after Laura died I was often distracted; it was hard to concentrate. The house was quiet with only one child, and it felt strange. There was such a huge difference in how our family felt. Colin didn't demand attention and I just wanted to enjoy him. He was my reason for making an effort every day. But that big energy of Laura's was gone from our lives, and the sadness was always there.

My mom and my dad were a great support to me while Laura was sick and after she died. Her death was so hard for them too. Their grief was for both me and for Laura. They were so sad to watch me grieve, and they were grieving themselves. She was very connected to Mom and Dad—they each played a specific and important role in her life. We were all in a terrible, uncontrollable state of grief. But we never stopped talking about Laura. She was always with us. Every one of us remembered stories of her escapades. She used to drive Colin crazy when she was little. He would have the Lego all set up in his bedroom and then I'd hear, "Mom, get her out of here." Or she would say some crazy little thing or swear, and he would just look at me and we'd roll our eyes.

There was a little boy named Jacob at daycare that Laura adored. She was three years old when she decided she was going to marry him. She was insistent on this and telling everyone. He was the most kind and gentle of all the children in the group, and I remember thinking, "Well, Laura, I hope your taste in men stays like this!" Another memory: when she was two, we were at a red light, a short red light, and she undid all the straps on her car seat, opened the back door of the car, and got out into the dark, pouring rain. Just because she decided to—and when she decided to do something, there were no other options. I was terrified she would be hit by a car! I got out, picked her up, strapped her back in and got to the next light. Not the best drive home.

Laura was a wild spirit and she had tremendous energy. I felt like she passed that energy to me. I tried to absorb it all, make it a part of me, keep it alive, and transpose it into something even better. I was inspired by what was probably inner willfulness, curiosity, and determination, but transformed into a powerful drive. I wanted to use that energy to honour her life. So when I started working at BC Children's Hospital, I took that energy plus everything I learned from my experience as a parent and used it in the work I did with children and families. Parents would sometimes say, "You really understand what I'm saying." And that was true because I had been there. Illness changes a child and it changes the family. Laura's illness and death made me a different person. It affected my beliefs and values; they grew stronger, deeper. I have always believed that children are persons and deserve to be treated with respect—even though it's sometimes difficult to do when their behaviour is hard to cope with.

Children must be able to trust those who provide care for them. A few minutes of really listening to a child, without distractions or another agenda, makes all the difference for them. Children can learn to adapt to very difficult situations, but giving them the gift of time and attention can make things so much easier. Sometimes it is the parents who need the most support, and it can be difficult for them to ask for help. Support systems like family and friends make a huge difference. Not all parents have that support, and still, they do the best possible job with what they have. I wanted to take Laura's energy and make a difference. I worked hard to bring everything I learned, everything I experienced with Laura, to help families as they coped with so many ups and downs. It was as if there was another dimension to my work. It was based not only on empathy for others but, really, on an understanding of how the dynamics of illness can affect the whole family.

My own concern for how Colin was coping with Laura's illness and, ultimately, her death always carried over into my concern for the siblings of sick kids. It was important for me that siblings who were in disequilibrium had someone listen to them and understand their situation. From time to time a parent would worry that a brother or sister was struggling, and I could step in with undivided attention to really listen and play and help them with whatever was on their mind. They needed that therapeutic play as much as the child who was sick. It wasn't necessarily meant to be a part of my job, but I believed it was really important. I always encouraged student interns in Child Life studies to work with siblings as well as the sick child, to look at their work with families in a more holistic way.

After I retired, I continued to bring that energy, Laura's energy, to my work with the Children's Heart Network (CHN). I was open with those families about my experience as a bereaved parent, and this helped build a trust with them. I understood what they were going through, and this made a difference to how we worked together. And I would think, "There you go, Laura. I did that because of you." Her presence was there in my beliefs, in my values. I'm not really a religious person or a spiritual one either. I don't believe in heaven and hell, but I do believe in honouring people. Working as I did, caring as I did, was my way of honouring Laura's memory.

I went to university full-time in the September after Laura died. I had wanted to go for a long time, and I was so happy to be there. I remember thinking, "I can be happy in different situations. I can laugh and tell jokes with my friends." But I didn't feel joy. I didn't feel it for years—that exuberance you can have in so many things you do. It was just gone. Still, being in class, being completely absorbed by something I loved, was the right thing for me. There were so many moments when I could relate the theories I was learning about to my life. It was an exciting time for me. And there were those other moments when I struggled to stay present, struggled to keep my grief at bay while I studied. But I persevered, channelling Laura's obstinance, perhaps, as well as her energy.

For the year Laura was sick and the next two years when I was at school, I was in "get it done" mode. After I graduated, I was hired at BC Children's Hospital. It meant leaving Victoria and moving to Vancouver. That mode of "get it done" continued as I made this huge move. I got things organized, packed up my home, and away I went. But when I look back, I don't really know *how* I did it. My friends helped me, and I'm sure my parents helped me; they must have paid for that moving truck because I had no money—just student debt! I had so many decisions to make. I was sad to leave Victoria, and setting things up in Vancouver was a big job. But I was excited about having a paycheque, a consistent paycheque that gave me a living wage. I was moving forward. It had been two years since Laura died, a milestone of sorts. Graduating from university and getting this new job helped me think that maybe things would be okay, that maybe I was actually competent. I had relied heavily on the support of friends and families in those two years, but now I felt ready to take on this new challenge. And I was lucky to find a new group of friends in Vancouver. My colleagues in the Child Life department became another nest of helpful, supportive people. We laughed so much together, especially during morning coffee, and it was good for me. They were just like my friends at home in no time.

What did I learn about myself in the months and years after Laura died? I learned that I was tough and that I could be happy. I was thirty-six years old when Laura died, and I was an immature thirty-six, a late bloomer (like Colin!). I didn't have the self-confidence I have now. I don't want awful things to happen to people, but bad things do happen, and when they do, I think it's a chance to learn something about ourselves. How do we adapt to situations? How can we support each other in hard times? I have learned that when challenges present themselves to me, I say "I can do it." I was afraid for my future and I doubted myself many times. I don't doubt anymore. I didn't believe in myself, and now I do. I learned that there was a place for me in the world, that I could be productive and helpful, and that gave meaning to my life. The death of my parents was sad, and I've lost friends, but Laura's death was the worst thing that ever happened to me. And I learned how to get through it.

I had nine months to adjust to what was happening to Laura when she was sick. Even though she suffered through the illness, it gave me time to prepare for her death. It was a horrible thing to watch but I couldn't, wouldn't, let it drag me down completely. Someone else's life was ending but it wasn't mine. I still had a life, and I knew I had to go on.

In 2007 there was a fire in my apartment building when I was out of town on holiday. Colin called to tell me he saw it on the morning news and went over to check on my building. My suite didn't burn, but a week later when I was able to return, I realized that the severe smoke and water damage meant it would be months before I could live in my home. I was so shattered that I couldn't go to work. I was so traumatized that I could barely sleep, and when I did sleep, I had terrible nightmares. I dreamed I was living in a subway station with both my children, homeless. I had recurring nightmares of finding Laura living in a hospital ward or lost somewhere else. I had dreams of finding her underwater, dead. I couldn't concentrate or complete tasks.

I needed professional help to figure out how to come back to myself. Fortunately, I found a great counsellor through my employer. Good friends offered me a room in their home, which was critical to my recovery. Unlike other times when I would stay with friends, I rarely made contributions in this household. I simply couldn't. I couldn't even cook, something I love to do. I felt homeless. The counsellor determined that I was suffering from PTSD [post-traumatic stress disorder], and the unresolved trauma came from a series of experiences including the end of my marriage and Laura's death. I never had time to deal with all the grief attached to those events, but after the fire I had no choice.

When I think about resilience, my grandmother immediately comes to mind. I loved and admired her. She immigrated to Canada from England in 1908 and married my grandfather the day she got off the train. He had emigrated three years earlier. Their first home was a little "soddy" (my mother and grandmother would be horrified if I called it a shack but . . . it kind of was!) just outside Raymore, Saskatchewan. I have a photograph of it, and I look at that picture almost every day. She moved from a comfortable home in England to that tiny home and she made it work. Looking at that picture reminds me of what she gave to me through her own sacrifice—to leave her home of comfort and face the unknown. I can make a direct comparison between her life and my own. She lost her first baby but went on to have three more children; my mom was the youngest. In about 1912 they moved from the farm into the little town of Raymore, where my grandfather started a horse-drawn freight business. In 1920, when Mum was four years old, her father died suddenly, leaving my grandmother alone with three children. She did everything she could to keep her family together.

My grandfather had built a new house in Raymore, and he still had his freight business when he died. She took the business over and continued to run it with the help of her eldest son and a hired man. The business thrived for several years until a fellow from another village started a new freight company, and all the men in town moved their business to him. Because the men moved their business away from my grandmother's company, she had only her savings from the business to live on. My mum grew up in a comfortable home, but there was definitely financial strain and a lot of careful budgeting. Grandma took in boarders, and eventually her eldest son began to work, helping his mother make ends meet. Times were tough but she managed. I learned how to manage too.

In 1920, women got the right to vote in Saskatchewan, so I believe the first election my grandmother voted in was in 1921. As the election drew nearer, various men started knocking on her door, all there to "instruct" my grandmother on who she should vote for now that she had the right to vote. She was insulted and incensed. She didn't need to be instructed by those men; she was very capable and able to think for herself. Years later she said to me, "You make up your own mind. You pay attention, you keep your head up, and you take advantage of what different situations bring your way."

Grandma never let herself sink into self-pity. She had three children to raise and she did a good job of it. When I have been in difficult situations or going through tough times, memories of my grandma helped me through. I would use self-talk to convince myself that if Grandma could feed three children, I could feed two. If Grandma could stand up to those pushy men, I could have confidence too. If she could live in a sod house, I could share a bedroom with two kids. If she could suffer a miscarriage on the open prairie, I could care for a sick child. She was my role model as a single parent. She had to adjust to the death of her husband because she had a family to care for. My grandfather was extroverted by nature while she was more reserved. Living without him must have been a lot like my strange adaptation to living without Laura. Her resilient nature was a beacon of light for me.

It had only been two years since Laura died when I started working at BC Children's Hospital. One of the greatest challenges that you face when you work in a children's hospital is the death of a child. And the first death I faced was very difficult. All I could think about was the parents' grief. I knew what was facing them, and I was deeply saddened for them. I worked there for twenty-two years and it was always that way. I was always so sad for the families. There were dozens of children who died over the years. I attended many funerals and I even spoke at some. It was always an awful situation for the parents. I knew they would face overwhelming waves of grief that come hour after hour and would continue month after month, year after year. My grief as a support person to that family was nothing compared to what that family was going through themselves. Each child's death brought back my own grief, but no matter what, I knew the sadness I was feeling for the family was so different from what they were experiencing. I was able to keep myself separate and out of that deep, deep kind of grief that each family suffered.

Life is full of surprises. I had goals in life like we all do, but when they actually happened, each time it was a surprise. Graduating from university was a surprise because I never thought I would be able to go to school. Getting my job at BC Children's Hospital was a wonderful surprise that allowed me to build a better life for Colin and for me. So many opportunities came along that validated me as a person and as a professional, like being asked to teach at a college in the Fraser Valley, the Delta School Board Early Childhood Education program, and the University of Victoria. I wrote a chapter for a book, I wrote manuals with colleagues, and I have been part of a team who wrote *Ethics in Child Life Practice*, the second edition of which will come out in spring 2021. These are accomplishments I never dreamed would happen. The best professional surprise was receiving a Lifetime Achievement Award in Family

Centered Care given to me by the Association of Child Life Professionals. To have the confidence of families, my peers, and colleagues has really validated my professional life and, in turn, my private life. And I think that being Colin and Laura's mother allowed me to be *that* person, the one who could help others and be proud of my contributions.

It took time to heal, but eventually I was well enough to go back to work, to resume my life. I learned through self-reflection to be aware of my state of mind and to take care of myself. In time, the joy that had been missing for so long started to re-emerge. I can't remember the exact moment—it could have been something as simple as watching Tessa Virtue and Scott Moir, the Canadian ice dance champions, skate at the 2010 Olympics. I remember watching them through my tears. I was so happy. It was like bursting out of a bubble. Joy. I could feel it again. It was a wonderful thing.

I have started to paint, and the happiness I feel when I am painting is a surprise. I painted a few things in art class at high school but not a lot. When I picked up a paintbrush in 2015 and put it to paper, good things started to happen. I was amazed. I spent so many years focused on trying to do things "right"—be a good daughter, be a good parent, be a good everything to everyone. I wanted an education, I wanted to purchase my own home. I wanted to pay the bills. And I worried about everything all the time. There was no time for things like painting. But when I picked up that brush, let the paint have its way, there were exciting results. "Happy accidents." And I love it.

I am sitting here, looking at the ocean. Every morning I look out and think, "How did this happen to me?" To sit and immerse myself in paint-ing for hours brings me joy. When I go out for a hike in the woods, I feel joy. Nature's unbelievably beautiful garden brings me joy. That feeling was lost for so long. I am seeing beauty again, and with that comes joy. It is back. I still have tears of sadness in my eyes when I think about Laura, and I can have tears of joy when I think about things of beauty. They live side by side. And I think, "We did it, Laura! I used that energy you passed to me and here I am." Surprise for sure!

Kim's Reflection

Diane Coutu says, "When we truly stare down reality, we prepare ourselves to act in ways that allow us to endure and survive extraordinary hardships" (p. 8). Bindy did this in every facet of her life, including the time leading up to Laura's death. Almost from the beginning, she faced the real possibility that Laura was going to die. As devastating as this was, Bindy didn't hide from the truth. Instead, she worked to make Laura's last months the best they could be. In our conversation, Bindy said, "I had nine months to adjust to what was happening to Laura when she was sick. Even though she suffered through the illness, it gave me time to prepare for her death. It was a horrible thing to watch, but I couldn't, wouldn't, let it drag me down completely. Someone else's life was ending but it wasn't mine. I still had a life, and I knew I had to go on."

Finding a reason to go on is tricky, but Victor Frankl reminded us how important it is to find meaning and purpose in the face of unimaginable loss. He said, "Life holds potential meaning under any conditions, even the most miserable." Bindy searched for that new meaning in her life even as she grappled with Laura's death, and she found it. She had a son, and he deserved to have a full life, even in the face of his sister's death. Focusing her energy on creating a meaningful life for Colin, a life filled with happiness—not one shrouded in loss—rekindled her desire to make her own life meaningful. Building a new life didn't negate Bindy's sorrow; she took that sadness with her every step of the way. But it didn't stop her from moving forward.

Bindy embraced another of the characteristics Diane Coutu references— resourcefulness. Coutu says that resilient people "make the most of what they have" (p. 13). Bindy had a community of friends she had built over the years. They were her most important resource. She reached out to them, and they became a lifeline during Laura's illness. Their generosity continued after Laura died, helping Bindy build a new life for Colin and for herself. Bindy's resourcefulness was essential as she moved to a new city, began a new job, and built a new community of friends.

When I interviewed Bindy, she told me she was sitting at her living room window, looking out toward the ocean. I had been to Bindy's home, so I could picture her sitting in her favourite chair with pictures of Laura and Colin on one table and a picture of her grandma's sod house on another.

Nothing could have made me happier. I watched her navigate rough waters over the years as she rebuilt a life without Laura. That promise she made to herself to use the mighty energy Laura passed to her came true in every facet of her life. I continue to marvel at Bindy's tenacity, and I think, "You are where you are meant to be, my friend, surrounded by beauty, filled with joy."

CHAPTER FOUR:
SHARON AND PAUL

In this chapter you will meet Sharon and Paul. Married for close to fifty years, they have two children, three grandchildren, and a quiet, contented life. Like most of us, they were doing their best to live a full life. And then cancer came calling. Not just to one of them but to both. These are their stories.

PART ONE—SHARON

Kim's Story

SHARON AND I MET IN JUNE 1999. *We were sitting next to each other in the third-floor student lounge at Royal Roads University in Victoria, BC. There was a very young man wittering away at us about the "rules and regulations" of life as a student in the university residence. Why? Because that is what we were—brand-new students. Mature students, if you will, but students nonetheless. We had both signed up to do our master's degrees. As he droned on, we looked at each other. Sharon spoke first. She said one phrase, which I would hear often over the next twenty-plus years: "What the fuck!"*

Our friendship grew quickly. It was deeply rooted in our goals, values, and beliefs about so many things: family, friends, education, community, and the need for connection and reflection. We studied together, ate meals together, shared many bottles of wine! We came to be a part of each other's families, even though we lived thousands of miles apart. We completed our studies and went on with our lives. But we stayed connected, and our friendship deepened as the years passed.

When Sharon called to tell me her cancer diagnosis, I didn't know what to say. It wasn't a long phone call, thank heaven. Sharon was my dear friend, and I had no idea how to help. So I did the only thing I could think of in the moment. I listened. Over the next year as she experienced multiple treatments, I bumbled along, relying on listening, not talking. I still didn't know what to say that would be of any help.

Sharon's strength of character, her incredible sense of humour, and her humility shone amid the tears, the fears, the fragile moments. Her resilience, tenacity, and marvellous sense of the absurd helped ease her journey through the crazy world of cancer. Cancer did define her for a little while; it doesn't now. But it did highlight what I already knew—she was more resilient than she believed. Now she knows. She is irrepressible.

Sharon's Story

I have cystic, lumpy breasts, and when I felt a lump in my breast, I thought it best to get it checked. I was a little overdue for a mammogram, so I made an appointment to see my GP. I told myself that everything would be fine. But in the back of my mind I wondered—is this cancer? I am a nurse, and I had some experience with cancer during my nursing career. Pictures of those people floated through my mind. And my mother died a horrible death from cancer at the age of fifty-seven. I was fifty-seven, and I did not want to die at that age.

I saw my doctor on Wednesday, September 21, 2011. She examined my breasts and said, "I want you to go to the Gattuso Rapid Diagnostic Centre for Breast Cancer at Princess Margaret Hospital [PMH] in Toronto." She told me she was concerned that the lump was cancer. The next day she phoned to tell me I had an appointment at PMH on Monday. I didn't tell my husband, Paul, about my doctor's appointment. He was in Florida on a golfing trip, and I thought, "What's the point? He can't help me right now." And the whole idea of possibly having cancer hadn't really hit me. I was still working, and that helped to distract me, helped me set aside my worries for the moment.

On September 26, 2011, I was at the Gattuso clinic for a mammogram. After the technician did the mammogram, she told me to come back to the clinic in the afternoon. She didn't say why, and I didn't ask. I said, "That's fine. I'll go grab some lunch and come back." I thought they probably wanted to do a breast ultrasound. It was a common practice when they wanted to double-check something, and I'd had this additional test in the past.

When I returned to the clinic after lunch, the receptionist said the nurse practitioner was looking for me. Before I could speak with the nurse practitioner, a different nurse came and told me they wanted to do an ultrasound, and they were ready for me. What I didn't know at that point was the mammogram had showed a fair-sized lump and they wanted to do a biopsy right away. They wanted the nurse practitioner to talk to me because they believed I had breast cancer. I never did speak to the nurse practitioner.

I went into the ultrasound room and a radiologist was waiting for me. She started poking my breast without even introducing herself. She said she was going to do a needle biopsy of the lump because she believed it was cancer. She didn't say anything else. Cancer. The radiologist, the nurse and the radiology tech had said that word to me so far that day, as if it was normal to throw it around, like it was no big deal. But it was a big deal, and as the radiologist jabbed at my breast, it sank in—oh my God, I have breast cancer. Fuck.

The biopsy was gruelling and painful. The tumour was calcified so it was difficult to obtain a sample. The radiologist inserted the needle four separate times before she was satisfied with the sample. She told me she thought the third try would be the last time. She was wrong—she had to go in again. I was so anxious, so fearful as I waited for the fourth needle to go in that without thinking I called out, "Bitch." She wrote in the report that I had an "inappropriate reaction" to having the biopsy. (That note in my file followed me throughout my entire treatment. Every doctor asked me about the incident.)

When the biopsy was over, all I wanted to do was get the hell out of the hospital, go back to work, collect my belongings, and go home. Paul was home from his trip by then and back at work. (He was a Toronto police officer.) I called him and told him that I had cancer. He was the first person I shared this news with. He picked me up and took me back to my job at the Centre for Addiction and Mental Health (CAMH). I had driven to work that day, so I needed to pick up my car.

When I got back to work, I told the director of the unit I was managing that I had breast cancer. She was supportive and kind. I let her know I wouldn't be back to work until the next Monday and would keep her apprised of the plan. I drove home by myself in a mental fog.

When I arrived home, I sat and talked with Paul about my diagnosis. We were both stunned. It was all so unbelievable. I called my daughter and my son. Then I called my two sisters and asked them to let my brother know. It was a difficult call to make. I knew it would be very hard for my siblings to hear I was sick. Our mother had died from cancer in 1988, and then our father died a year later of heart failure. We lost our youngest brother to AIDS in 2002. And now I was ill.

I called a few close friends, and then I stopped. I was done for the day—a day that seemed to go on and on. Finally, I slept. I was exhausted. The next day my doctor phoned and confirmed what we already knew—the biopsy result was breast cancer. When she said, "This is cancer," I could feel my world, my whole world, come apart. Even though I had told people I had breast cancer, that phone call, that definitive confirmation statement, left me breathless. What do I do now? What does this mean for me? She said I had an appointment on Thursday, September 28 with a surgical oncologist. I feel really lucky that I didn't have to spend much time in the place of fear and uncertainty about what was going to happen next.

When Paul and I saw the surgeon, he was very clear about what we needed to do, saying, "We have work to do over the next year." Before I left that appointment, my surgery to have the lump removed was booked for November 1. The nurse practitioner set some expectations around next steps, timelines post-operatively, and how the pathology report would determine what came next—more surgery, radiation, chemotherapy, or a combination of any of the three. She took her time setting time frames and what I could expect. She outlined the process, saying it would likely take approximately ten months after my initial surgery to complete the chemo and radiation. There was so much information, and I came away in shock. In that moment I thought, "No, this isn't really happening. This is a dream." The next moment I thought, "It's real. This really is happening to me; it really is happening to me."

With my surgery set for November 1, 2011, I needed to finish up my contract work for CAMH as the manager on the Dual Diagnosis unit. We were in the process of hiring a manager as it was, and I would have only about a week to do some orientation with her. I had moments of feeling like I was on the outside looking in, just going through the motions. It was hard to be mentally present at work with surgery, chemotherapy, and radiation facing me. I did what I absolutely had to do, and I did my best. I would like to have done more orientation with the new manager, but there wasn't time with my surgery date looming. I am a bit of a perfectionist, so it was hard to leave without finishing everything perfectly. But I had to let go of that ideal and get ready to face the next hurdle. I chose to surrender, doing the best I could in that moment. It was clear to me that care for myself was the priority if I was going to survive cancer.

It was a long road, especially in the early days when I didn't know what steps would follow next. After my first surgery I focused on healing and resting. A number of family and friends dropped by for visits and to help around the house. At my two-week post-operative appointment with the surgical oncologist, we were told that there were cancer cells in my sentinel lymph node biopsy, and the tumour was stage 3. It had grown since my mammogram and breast MRI. The oncologist recommended that I have a lymph node resection after I finished chemo and before I started radiation. I asked for a referral to Southlake Regional Cancer Centre. I wanted to complete my chemotherapy and radiation treatments there because it was much closer to home, making travel back and forth easier.

A few weeks later we met with the oncologist at Southlake. Paul and my daughter, Clare, came to that first appointment with me for support and to ask their questions. I learned that my tumour was positive for estrogen and progesterone receptors, which guided the type and dosages of the chemotherapy I would receive. The oncologist recommended six chemo sessions scheduled every three weeks. They would begin on December 22, 2011. He was optimistic that with these treatments and radiation I would have a normal life expectancy. This made me feel hopeful, that going through this process would be worth it.

I had lots of emotions coming and going. Lots of fear about the unknown and about loss of control. At the time it felt like everyone had an opinion about what I should do, and I questioned my decisions from time to time. It was hard to know what to do. Throughout the process, Paul and the kids were incredibly supportive. The kids checked in regularly with me. I remember hanging out with Clare and doing movie night. Another time, my son, Eric, dropped by with his boss's brand-new Jaguar and took me for a ride. Paul came with me to all my chemotherapy treatments, and he was always there to help with anything I needed. Friends brought food, drove me to radiation treatments, sent cards, flowers, gifts, and lots of love. My sister-in-law Pat, who is a breast cancer survivor, encouraged me to be gentle and kind to myself. She sent me a book titled *Just Get Me Through This: A Practical Guide to Coping with Breast Cancer* by Deborah A. Cohen and Robert M. Gelfand MD, which she had found helpful when she was in treatment. Small gestures of kindness like Pat's made a big difference. And in the early days, hanging out with my dogs and being in nature gave me a healing place for my body and soul. I have an affinity for trees so I kept up daily walks as much as I could. It made a difference. I am not sure why—it just did.

I didn't think about dying, about my mortality. I didn't have time. I am sure it was there, in my subconscious somewhere, but there were too many other things to think about. When you are on this journey, it is like a job. With all the appointments and things to do to manage the side effects, you get into what I call "worker mode." My first three chemo sessions were not too bad. Yes, I lost my hair, lost my appetite, had brain fog, and was fatigued for the first week after a chemo treatment. Then I would have a couple of weeks of feeling pretty good. I did some contract work for the dual diagnosis management team at CAMH during those times.

I believe the underlying fear of dying drove me until my fourth chemo-therapy treatment. There was never really any talk about dying because you are fighting to live. As I prepared for the fourth round of chemo, I was still thinking of cancer as the enemy, the thing that invaded my body. It was something outside of me. The culture in our health care system promotes the notion that we have to *fight* cancer. The language we use, specific words and phrases, reinforce this perception. It is a *Battle*. And I was always on guard. I was always trying to figure out the answers to the constant chorus of questions like—Why did I get this cancer? What did I do wrong? What could I have done differently in my life? There was a sense of shame and I wondered, "Is it my fault I have cancer?" Shame and cancer are like sisters joined at the hip. As a woman, I thought I did something wrong. I didn't take care of myself, I ate the wrong food or drank too much alcohol, didn't exercise enough, and on it goes.

In my fourth chemotherapy session, they introduced a new cocktail of drugs, and my body just went "Oh my God. What have you done now?" One of the side effects of the drug cocktail was that it irritated every nerve in my body. It felt like someone was sticking pins in me, pins that carried fire into every part of me. I had pain in my nose, my tongue, my ears, my hands. My whole body was filled with pain; any movement was agony. Any thought of food was totally disgusting. Then constipation set in and my whole body just felt like it was tied up into a tight ball. This fourth treatment left me more fatigued than I thought I could ever be, and yet, I couldn't sleep. At that point I wasn't fearing death anymore. I was fearing life. Feeling like this treatment process wasn't worth it. I remember thinking, "If I could die, this would be a good time. If this is what the quality of my life is going to be—I am done."

Because I wasn't sleeping, I had lots of time to think in those long, dark hours before dawn. At some point during one of my pre-dawn sessions in the week after that fourth treatment, I realized that the more anxious I got about everything leading up to and including my treatments, the worse my pain was. So I decided I needed to do something differently, find a different way to get through my chemo treatments. I had to let go of my anxiety.

At that time, I was reading *Dying to Be Me* by Anita Moorjani. She struggled with lymphoma for four years, and in February 2006, she was in end-stage lymphoma. She was unconscious and ready to die, and she tells the story of leaving her body and seeing her family around her bed grieving. She describes an out-of-body experience in which her spirit met her father, who had already passed. He told her it was not her time and that she needed to return to her body as she had work to do in the world. She woke from her unconscious state and told her family she would be okay; she wasn't dying yet. Within five weeks she was cancer-free, and the doctors still don't know why. It was her belief that cancer was the challenge that saved her life. She said she was killing herself by trying to live up to other people's expectations, and her belief was she was never enough. She talks about cancer as a teacher. That was her message to me too. I needed to take care of myself, to let go of my own expectations and others' expectations that didn't serve me. It was one of many lessons I learned along the way.

One of the other things I remember from her book was her observations about the health care system, about how the culture of health care reinforces the idea that we need to fight our disease. You hear war words all the time when people talk about cancer, like "I beat it" or "You need to fight." I realized that my anxiety was tied to this need to fight my cancer. It was as if the health care system was teaching me how to fight when what I really needed to do was learn how to heal. As a nurse I probably had a better understanding of the risk involved in treating versus not treating my cancer. Treatment is a gamble—painful, with the possibility of long-term side effects. But having no treatment can bring you abruptly face to face with your mortality. I had to figure out a different way to manage how to move forward.

And so I made a conscious decision to put my energy into healing; to stop fighting. I needed to love myself to heal, and that meant my whole self, including my cancer. I needed to love my cancer because it was part of me. I am sure that this idea may be difficult for people to understand if they haven't faced cancer, but it made complete sense to me. Cancer didn't happen *to* me; it *was* me, my body. It was a negative energy in my body, and I didn't want it there. It didn't belong anymore. So instead of fighting it, I embraced it, loved it, and that helped me to love myself. I had forgotten how to love myself—I don't think I was very good at self-love, but it became very important to figure out. I was reminded of the saying, "We become what we think about." When I let go of the thoughts of fighting or battling cancer, I felt an immediate shift in my body. A whole new sense of calm came over me. My pain diminished almost immediately when I chose to focus on healing instead of fighting.

I did finish the last two chemo treatments. The oncologist reduced the dosages of the chemo cocktail by 10 percent. The side effects were still difficult—I lost my toenails and have permanent neuropathy in my feet. But I had changed. My attention now centred on healing and it felt good.

In April of 2012 I finished chemotherapy, and I had the lymph node resection in early May. In June, Clare and I met with the radiation oncologist. He recommended thirty radiation treatments starting once the incision from my lymph node resection was healed. He also suggested having a mastectomy. I found this troubling and said this was a decision between myself and the surgeon. I had a conversation with the surgical oncologist in September of 2012 about the additional surgery. He was satisfied that he had good margins for the tumour, and he did not recommend a mastectomy. It felt like the right decision to me as well. Such relief!

At the time of my diagnosis, a good friend started her shamanic training as a healer and asked if I would be her practice client. A couple of years prior to this, I had explored shamanism as a practice that could complement my Circle Practitioner work. A Circle Practitioner creates a safe space for conversations. It is not like facilitation, where you are directing the conversation. In Circle Practice, we sit together in a circle, and I act as a host, guiding people in a lightly held social structure. People share stories that help them make sense of their world. I might offer a prompt or a question that helps the conversation move forward, but the conversation is really guided by the participants. One person speaks at a time, often using a talking piece. This talking piece signals to the group that that particular person is the only one who can speak. Everybody else simply listens and witnesses the individual's story. Gathering like this helps people to slow down and listen differently, to listen deeply to each other. It is a way that helps build connections and community differently than other kinds of gatherings or meetings. We use a pause as needed to allow space between stories, and no one interrupts or speaks over anyone in the group. Circle has its origins in Indigenous community practices, so being in Circle rests deeply in our human DNA.

Similarly, shamanism is an ancient universal practice that has gained popularity in the last forty years around the world. The fundamental belief is that we are changing all the time, and shamanism honours this change process by bringing harmony to an individual. Shamanism is a spiritual practice, not a religion. It is aligned with, and comes from, Indigenous spiritual practices, where it is believed that all living things are related and have influences on our lives. Shamans believe when you have cancer, you are not aligned spiritually. They work with people to help realign your spiritual Self.

Working with a Shaman was an intuitive response; it just felt right. The medical care I was receiving focused on the physical piece of my body and that wasn't enough. If I was going to work towards healing, I needed harmony between my body and soul through a spiritual practice. Working with a Shaman was my first step. It was the first of several alternative health practices that I used in my healing journey.

In the beginning I met with the Shaman once a week. Each session started by opening a sacred space. (This is when one invites the spirits of our ancestors and all our relations—the sun, earth, animals, birds, all the plants, rocks, etc., to come into the energetic space to help what needs to be released, returned, and healed.) Then we would have a conversation about what I was coming to see her about that day—if I was angry or sad about something, for example, if there was something that needed to be resolved or maybe just talked about. Then she would use a crystal to check the level of energy in each chakra. There are seven chakras or energy points in the body, and if your energy is not flowing freely in each of the seven chakras, your whole body will be impacted. Simply put—you are feeling "off." The Shaman would guide me through a breathing exercise to open the blocked areas. I came away feeling calmer, grounded, a sense of wholeness, and more connected to the world around me.

As time went on, she performed what she called "soul retrieval." I had suppressed pieces of my soul for any of a host of reasons, from trauma, grief, etc. One soul that returned was a young child who was playful and happy; another was an Indigenous girl riding a horse. They always came with a message. She told me my spirit guide is Eagle, and every time she opens sacred space an eagle comes and sits on my shoulder. After a year of these sessions, I was feeling much stronger and not needing to see her as often. I still go a couple of times a year to release any energy blocks I may have accumulated.

I also did work with an energy healer who I knew, Denis Chagnon. I still see him periodically. In 1989, the doctors told him to get his life in order, he would be dead in a few months. He said that as he lay dying, he could feel energy from his hands on his abdomen healing his body. Even though the doctors tell you that cancer cells will always linger so you can never say you are cured, he believed he was cured. He said it was healing energy that came from his spirit. After he healed from his cancer, he felt called to become a healer for other people. He started a practice outside of Ottawa and came to Toronto once a month. He had me lie on a massage table, and he would put his hands on my shoulders, channelling healing energy into my body. He could sense if there was an energy blockage, and when he felt a blockage, he placed his hands on that area in my body. After a few minutes he would cover me up with a blanket and leave me for about twenty to thirty minutes. He would ask me to put my hands on my lower abdomen during that quiet time and ground my energy through my hands. When he returned, he repeated the process of channelling energy and told me how my energy was flowing. Sometimes I felt a little light-headed or dizzy but would recover in a few minutes. Generally, I felt good at the end of my sessions. I like to see him once or twice a year now. I have sent several people to him over the years who have found him to be very helpful in their healing process.

Body image plays an interesting role when you have cancer. During chemo I spent a lot of time in the bathtub just really relaxing, trying to rest my body and rid it of all the toxins from chemo. And so I saw a lot of myself. I lost all my hair, and that was frustrating because it never grew back, never looked like it did before I had cancer. I used to have a lot of hair, but I've grown to accept the new look. I don't look at the back much where it is thinner! Many women have reconstructive breast surgery when they lose part or all of a breast. My surgeon offered it to me, but I declined. I said, "You know what, it's fine. It's not that important to me." He said, "You're entitled to some vanity, and it's up to you." My boobs are not that much different; there's one that's smaller. I figured it was easier to just buy a good bra. I have known other women who had reconstructive surgery, and it was never a simple day-surgery fix. Some have complete reconstructive surgery for a double mastectomy, and it is a good eighteen to twenty-four months of multiple surgeries and a lot of pain. I know one young woman who had at least six surgeries for her reconstruction. In the end I was glad I chose not to have surgery. My scars remind me of how lucky I am to be here.

I learned to speak up for myself, to make decisions that felt right for me. I felt like a deer in the headlights at the beginning. I didn't know what questions to ask, and the medical team didn't give up a lot of information. In the beginning it was as if they were doing their work to me instead of for me and with me. They didn't consult with me, talk to me. And because of that, I went through unnecessary pain. Chemo was much more difficult than it needed to be. They didn't do an assessment of my veins to see if they were strong enough to take the drugs. I could have told them if they asked but they didn't. They ended up having to flush my veins with IV fluids, and I felt sicker from all the IV fluids than the chemo drugs. If they had just talked to me, told me their plans, it could have been easier for all of us. But over time, we started to work together.

Another situation that stands out was a confrontation with a resident. I was uncertain about having the lymph node resection because I didn't want to have another surgery. The resident talked down to me, talked about my body like it was a piece of meat. He said, "We will take a slab of tissue where the lymph nodes are." He assumed that I had already agreed to have the surgery, like I didn't have any choice. He was giving me orders, telling me what to do. I told him I wasn't having surgery based on the information he provided and asked him to leave. Paul and Clare were with me, and they were trying to talk me into having the surgery while we waited for the surgical oncologist to come. It was one of the few times when I didn't feel supported by Paul and Clare. I felt ashamed for thinking about not having the surgery. They both said I should do everything I could to prevent a recurrence, but it wasn't about them; it was about me. I am sure they were afraid I was going to die from breast cancer if I didn't have the surgery, but in that moment it wasn't supportive. I had every right to question having the surgery. My doctor came in, answered my questions, and gave me the option of not doing the surgery. He said that if I didn't have the surgery, he would follow me every three months to see how I was doing. I did decide to have the surgery, but I walked away from that appointment feeling defeated and very much alone. In the end, good things came out of the bad experiences like that one. I learned to speak up in ways I hadn't done before, particularly with members of the health care team. And at times, with my family. I pushed back, and I stood up for myself.

I have learned to take better care of my body. I continue to do my Feldenkrais, a practice that teaches you to move your body like you did when you were a child. It is one of my favourite classes. I am much more aware of how I move, and I have learned new movements that have helped my body heal and stay strong as I age. My Feldenkrais teacher is at least seventy years old, and watching her move is like watching a dancer. I always feel renewed, refreshed, at the end of a class. My body is aligned once again. And I walk my dogs every day, take them to various classes and attend dog shows from time to time. I was doing yoga and meditation before my diagnosis, and I continue to go to yoga once a week as well as meditation. I have found that meditation really helps me during MRIs. I just picture myself somewhere else, like a beach! And I have a job that I love. My job has allowed me to deepen my Circle Practice, helping the teams in my organization work more effectively together.

Travelling the cancer journey pushed me to focus on what was important and to let go of things that held me back, things that did not feed my heart. Each of these activities has helped me heal. Mind, body, and spirit.

I have changed in other ways as well. I really appreciate every moment. I am in less of a hurry. I notice things, small things, that passed me by before, like finding a bird's feather and wondering about the bird—where did it come from and where is it now? I use my daily dog walks as my walking meditation of the day. Being in the beauty of nature with no preconceived expectations helps me ground my body and soul, to be open and curious about what is next.

The walk with cancer is an individual path. It is very difficult not to default to pressure from family and the health care system. But you must remember that you get to choose what you want to do. I've seen many people choose to do different treatments and they're still here with us today. I had a lumpectomy, lymph node resection, radiation, and chemotherapy. Another woman chose radiation followed by surgery but no chemo. Another woman couldn't tolerate chemotherapy and had enough strength and fortitude to say, "No more right now." In the end, she had to have a double mastectomy and reconstructive surgery because of the kind of cancer she had. But in that earlier moment, she took the break she needed. Everybody's story is different and it's a singular path. And it can be lonely sometimes. I had to learn what worked for me and say it out loud. I learned to be kind to myself, and to reach for the support when I needed it. I didn't go to support groups because I had a really supportive network, but they are there for people who need them. Alternative health options can also be very helpful. There is no one right way.

I felt disconnected from life at times during my cancer treatments, and so I loved all the cards that came. They were something to look forward to—they made me feel cared for and they reconnected me to the world. I did regular updates on email when I was going through treatment. It was helpful for me to write about what was happening, and it gave me a way to stay in touch without expending my limited energy. I have boxes of journals that I'll probably burn someday, but at the time, writing was important. I found it very cathartic. Another valuable thing people did was simply listen to me. They didn't try to fix the situation (they couldn't anyway!); they just let me talk. And other times, they accepted that I didn't want to talk. I was living with cancer and everything that came along with it. I was careful about how many phone calls I took. Sometimes I just didn't want to talk and that was okay.

There were surprises along the way as well, good surprises. I think of them as gifts that came out of this experience. The most important one—I got my soul back. It is difficult to put into words because feelings can be like that sometimes. You just have to accept that when I say I have my soul back, it means I am whole again. And if I ever get cancer again or something else, I know the healing won't be about *fighting*. I will settle into "it," whatever "it" turns out to be, first. Then I will figure out what's going to work versus going through that whole mechanistic way of thinking. I think when you have lived through cancer treatments and navigating the medical care system, you learn a lot about yourself from the perspective of what you would do differently if the time comes again. In the beginning, everything moved so fast—it was a whirlwind of emotions and fear. I came away with some wisdom about how to live. I will play the game of life until the day arrives for my passing. That was a huge gift for me.

I realized that I needed to be with people as well. I love my alone time, but I needed a circle of people to walk with me. The journey to wellness is lonely and it can be all-consuming. I needed to connect to something else besides my cancer. Being with people helped me stay connected to that bigger world. I received the gift of deeper friendships with the women in my life. Of course, I had friends before, but now the connections with many of them are much deeper. I love the men in my life, but the relationship with my woman friends is just different. I am not sure I can trust many men with my heart. This comes with my ongoing learning about how women are socialized, talked over, ignored, considered anomalies or exceptional if one is successful, smart, etc. At this stage in my life my tolerance for the bullshit is pretty low. Heart to me is about my soul/spirit. Women have been more open to listening, holding my vulnerability and honesty without judging it.

I am kinder to myself and less judgmental of others. Everyone has a story they carry of trauma, loss, and problems. I have learned that my thoughts are energy, and they impact me and the world around me. When I am grateful for the lessons learned on my cancer journey, I am better able to listen to myself and others. I continue to learn and stretch in the work I am doing now. In 2011 my work was not feeding my heart. I did good work as a manager, but I was repeating old patterns, working in a toxic environment with thankless administrative work, budgets, performance reviews that left little time to support the staff. My cancer gave me no choice but to close the door on that kind of work and focus on my own health. I didn't want to be a manger anymore. I wasn't sure what I wanted to do, but 2011 was a threshold moment. No looking back.

I always thought I was a strong person, but I learned that I am stronger, much stronger, than I believed. I think my resilience comes from the belief that life is the journey, and the moment I am in is what really matters. I probably first articulated that life is a process when I was deep in a big transformation change project with the Ontario Nurses Association. That whole project was a huge learning time as we tore down the existing structures and procedures and recreated the organization. I learned that every day my feet land on the floor is a day of possibility.

My resilience was something I learned early on in life. I was the oldest of five children, and our family, like many families, was dysfunctional. I was given lots of responsibility early, including the care of my siblings. My parents' resources were limited and there was substance and physical abuse between them. I left home when I was eighteen years old. I had the foresight to apply for a student loan to attend nursing school, and I had a summer job. I had a lingering sense that things would fall apart if I didn't take care of myself. But that threshold, that new beginning, showed me I just might make it in life. I knew it was important for me to leave my family home to thrive and not just survive. I am sure in those moments I could not have articulated this; I just knew in my heart that I needed to leave. Trusting my heart, trusting my intuition, and that faith in myself, that was my resilient Self guiding me forward.

The sun came out today and the snow is melting; my heart is full.

Kim's Reflection

Sharon is a remarkable, caring woman who rediscovered her resilience through her illness. Her strength had been tested frequently over the years, but this time was different. Cancer came with an urgency Sharon had not felt before. She chose to embrace the disease instead of fighting it, believing that was the only way she could build a new life worth living. Paul describes Sharon as "an exceptionally strong person," and she learned in the early days of her illness that she would need to pull that strength inward, using it to take care of herself. That was where her resilience lay.

Sharon had begun the inner journey of rediscovering herself in the years leading up to her diagnosis. She did meditation and yoga, and she found work that she loved. These pieces of her life helped settle a restlessness that I had seen in her for many years. The new practices she embraced calmed her, as did her love of the outdoors. They combined in a way that awoke a new aspect of her spirit. These practices became beacons of light on her road to recovery and continued to give her strength to care for Paul.

Stockdale and Frankl stressed the importance of finding new meaning in life because when you find that meaning, you have hope. As a nurse, Sharon knew what lay ahead when she received her cancer diagnosis. Like Stockdale, she faced the brutal reality, but also like him, accepting her situation didn't mean giving up. She continued looking ahead, reaching for life. She believed she had more to do. Even on the most difficult days, Sharon pushed herself forward so that on the less difficult ones she could embrace the things that gave meaning to her life. The approach seemed to be working!

But then Paul got sick. Where would the next wave of resilience come from for Sharon? Or would it come? Anyone who knows Sharon would scoff at the idea that she wouldn't rise to the occasion, but she doubted herself. She was tired.

Sharon went with Paul to the doctors and the first round of treatment. Being present for the next rounds became difficult. There were too many reminders of her own illness. However, the years spent building her self-awareness and her understanding of how to care for herself were Sharon's salvation. She drew on that knowledge so she could care for him and, at the same time, care for herself. The trees became her refuge once again, allowing her to settle her spirit, regain her equilibrium, and be fully present with Paul when he really needed her. Once again she called on the same spirits that Frankl, Stockdale, and others did so that she could face the reality of the day and still be hopeful for the future.

Research studies across the world have validated what Sharon learned intuitively—nature heals the soul. As Frank Lloyd Wright, the great American architect, said, "Study nature, love nature, stay close to nature. It will never fail you." Sharon continues to seek out nature to rekindle her own strength so that she can handle the difficult days.

Sharon's has been a remarkable journey of resilience. As Paul continues to face multiple bouts of cancer, Sharon stands quietly beside him. This poem speaks to her intimate understanding of where her strength lies and what she must do "when facing a fact that cannot be changed" (Frankl).

PART TWO — PAUL

Kim's Story

Paul and I met in the spring of 2001. His wife, Sharon, and I had just completed our master's degrees, and Paul came to Vancouver from Toronto for our graduation. I had seen pictures of Paul and he looked quite tall, but when I met him—wow! He was a big person. I looked like an eight-year-old standing next to him. He bent over and gave me a hug that engulfed my whole body. As he hugged me, his face broke into a huge smile, and I was instantly captivated. He was kind, funny, and when he laughed, his whole body laughed. And to this day, whenever I see him, that same smile lights his face. Sharon and I have stayed close friends over the years, and Paul is right there, standing next to her. They have been together for over forty years and I have known them for over twenty.

Paul radiated health. He had managed a couple of health hurdles over the years, but for as long as I had known him, he was well. He supported Sharon through her cancer treatments, doing all he could to encourage her. He was the rock. She leaned on him, knowing that no matter what, his strength would help carry her back to good health. That is who he is— dependable, caring. Strong and robust.

And then, one day, the doctor called. It was the summer of 2016.

Paul's Story:

When I was on the Toronto police force, I participated in a study regarding colon cancer. I had to have a physical examination and a colonoscopy. The purpose was to develop a blood test to detect the disease. This study was done approximately eighteen years ago, so I wasn't surprised when I received a postcard from my doctor's office, explaining that it was time for me to have a fecal matter test. My doctor said, "It's routine because of your age" (I was sixty-two at the time). I had to put a little bit of fecal matter on the card, seal it, and mail it off to the lab. That was it. I dropped it into the mailbox and forgot about it.

I got a call from my doctor about ten days after I mailed off that card. He said, "You need to come in and see me." People don't usually get a direct call from their family physician. So away I went to my family doctor the very next day. He referred me to a surgeon who did colonoscopies.

I phoned the surgeon's office as soon as I got home. He works at the big hospital, Markham Stouffville, but he also has a clinic in Uxbridge, a small town near me. Lo and behold, he had an opening at the Uxbridge clinic. I went to the clinic and met with the surgeon. He told me that there was blood in the fecal matter, and he wanted to do both a colonoscopy and an endoscopy. They wanted to look in my stomach, intestines, and colon. He said he routinely looked at everything. He was also interested in my past history of stomach ulcers. He was concerned that I could possibly have stomach cancer. So about ten days later, I had all the tests done.

Up until this point I had been feeling okay, but as I walked into the clinic for my colonoscopy, I realized that I really didn't feel well. I thought, "This isn't good." I've had all sorts of experience with family members, close relatives, and friends dropping off like flies from cancer, and immediately I went to a bad place. When Sharon was diagnosed with breast cancer, I felt numb. I was frustrated that I couldn't do anything to change the results, to make it better for her. And now here I was, and I thought, "This is a place where I don't have any control of the outcome."

They didn't use a lot of anaesthetic for the procedure so they wouldn't have a hard time waking me up. The first thing the doctor said to me was, "Your stomach's a bit inflamed. We can give you some medication for that." The second thing he said was, "And by the way, you have colon cancer." I said, "Okay." But it wasn't okay. It hit me like a hammer, and I immediately started thinking, "How much time do I have?" I wasn't thinking straight, and I was not feeling positive. Luckily, my wife, Sharon, was with me. Her support was crucial.

Although the doctor was a little abrupt, he was reassuring. He had a great bedside manner. He said he would be able to operate and take care of things, but more tests were needed. I had to complete a full day of pre-operative testing at Markham Stouffville Hospital in preparation for surgery. He instructed me to contact his office for an appointment so that he could go over the plan of action. When I got home, I checked him out. I talked to a few people I knew in the health system, and it was clear that he was very qualified. I felt confident he could do the job.

When I saw the doctor the second time, it was in his office. It was much easier to talk to him there. And I also felt more at ease because Sharon was with me. She asked questions and took notes. He talked about how early detection of colon cancer decreased the chance of dying—lots of talk about percentages. We talked about the surgery he would do, depending on what he saw when he operated. He explained that the extent of the cancer would dictate if he would need to resection the colon. He also talked about the possibility of a full recovery or the need for a colostomy. It was all pretty overwhelming, but leaving the office, I was still feeling confident that I had a good doctor.

Waiting for the surgery was difficult. I wanted it all over immediately, but I had to wait. Four weeks after the colonoscopy, I had a colon resection, which is a major surgery. The surgeon informed me that the cancer had perforated the wall of the colon. Because of the perforation I would need some form of radiation and possibly chemotherapy. This was not good news. He also explained that the resection was very tricky to do because of the location. He said they actually used a staple gun to put things back together. And he said, "You are lucky I have small hands because I completed the job suturing by hand." He seemed quite pleased with himself. I was in the hospital for five days and then I went home to continue my recovery. There was still a long road ahead.

I was referred to an oncologist, but I didn't see him for about seven weeks after the surgery. They needed to wait until I was healed from surgery before they began any kind of treatment. I still wasn't feeling good when I went to see the oncologist, and I didn't know why. Everyone thought I should be better. When I did see him, he laid out a plan for me, told me everything was going to be fine. He reassured me a hundred times in different ways. But I had reservations. It wasn't that I didn't believe him—I just had reservations. And it turned out that I was right to be concerned. When I look back, he came across like a snake oil salesman. His plan was six chemotherapy treatments and possibly radiation. Sharon was with me during our office visit, taking notes. She was trying to reassure me that everything would work out, but (I found out much later) she didn't like the guy either. As it turns out, I had reason to be concerned about the doctor. After the fourth treatment he said to me, "You have only four to go." I confronted him, saying, "You told us only six treatments." Sharon had made copious notes during the office appointment, so I knew what he had said, but he denied it.

I went through the first set of treatments—eight rounds of chemo every three weeks. I remember walking to our car in the parking lot after the first treatment. I said to Sharon, "We better hurry, I can feel ice pellets hitting my face." But it wasn't ice pellets; my stinging face was a side effect. The nerves in my face had become hypersensitive to anything cold. The same thing happened to my fingers. They had become so sensitive that touching anything cold was excruciating. Sharon bought me a package of insulated gloves at Costco so I could pick up cold things from the fridge and freezer. That was just one of many side effects that I experienced over the next months.

I started chemotherapy in November 2016 and completed it March 2017. When I went back to see the oncologist at the end of the chemo sessions, he actually said, "You are cured; you are good to go." Well, even though I was still feeling the side effects of chemotherapy, I felt like Jesus—I was walking on air. It's like I was flying. I was cured! I had a follow-up appointment with him for January 2018 but I cancelled it. I was finished with that guy, and besides—I was cured. Why go back?

I developed respiratory problems during my chemo. I thought it was simply a side effect, like the feeling of ice pellets. But in February 2018 things were getting worse. I had a cough and post-nasal drip. My sinuses were really bothering me, and I thought, "I need to see my family physician." I really liked him. He was young, smart, and he paid attention to his patients. He listened to my chest and said, "There is something going on here. Your chest sounds terrible, and I want to make sure you don't have pneumonia." He sent me to the local hospital to have an Xray. It took just a matter of minutes to get there, and I had to wait less than four minutes. I thought, "Great—I can go!" No one said I needed to wait for results, and so away I went. Sharon and I had somewhere to be that evening, and she was waiting for me. I whipped home, picked her up, and off we went.

Less than an hour after the X-ray, Sharon and I were still driving when my cell phone rang. It was the family doctor. He said, "We have a problem here. There's something in the left lower lobe of your lung." The hospital called him as soon as they read the X-ray, and right away, he called me. When I hung up the phone, I wasn't feeling very good! You don't have to be a rocket scientist to figure that this mass in my lung wasn't a coincidence. I thought it definitely had to be associated with the original colon cancer. This turned out to be true, but it was a while before I knew for sure. I had a lung biopsy done in March 2018 and this confirmed it was cancer. The perforation of the bowel in the original surgery allowed the cancer to spread. And here we were—the beginning of the second round with cancer.

I wasn't pleased about anything at this point. I certainly wasn't pleased with the oncologist who had treated me. He had declared me cured, and yet here I was with a mass in my lung. I went and saw my family doctor a few days after he called. We had a good discussion and I told him that I didn't want to be referred back to the facility that handled my colon cancer. I wanted to go somewhere else. He referred me to the clinic that Sharon had gone to for her cancer treatment. I was happy about that.

I got an appointment within fourteen days after the X-ray. I saw a different oncologist and a radiologist who specialized in cancer treatment. The radiologist was fantastic. She explained that she didn't feel I required radiation, but she was going to double-check with her colleagues. In the end they decided that the best course of action was no radiation at that time. They were a good team, and I was well taken care of.

Because I had this mass in my lung, the oncologist wanted me to see a thoracic surgeon. Up until this point in my life, I'd had very few surgeries. I had my tonsils out when I was eleven years old and three major surgeries as an adult. So, to be honest, when I saw the thoracic surgeon, I was very apprehensive. I wasn't thinking that I was going to see the Pearly Gates, but I was worried about what was coming. He said he wasn't sure how much of my lung he would have to remove and wouldn't know until he was operating. I thought, "Well, this is just great! Jesus—how much of my lung are they going to have to take out?" Thankfully, they only had to take a small part. It worked out in the end, but I was not happy about any of it. I kept on thinking that this shit really shouldn't be happening at all. It should have been taken care of right the first time. I was angry when I found myself back in surgery because the cancer hadn't been taken care of properly from the start. I told the thoracic surgeon I was not happy with the oncologist from Markham Stouffville Hospital. I believed that the cancer should have been taken care of in the first surgery. He said he couldn't honestly say if it would have made a difference; the cancer might have returned anyway.

And I was angry that I was going to put my wife through this again. We had gone through colon cancer surgery and twenty-four rounds of chemo. But here we were again, facing more surgery, more chemo. I thought, "Great, here we go again." And it didn't need to be this way. I felt like a burden to Sharon. I was going to be laid up again and she was going to have to take care of me, again. Sharon was very reassuring, reminding me that I was there for her when she had chemo, but honestly, I still felt badly.

One of the biggest things that helped me move forward was the straightforwardness of my health providers. Most of the doctors and the nurses were all straight shooters. I didn't feel like I was being hood-winked or coddled, like someone had to hold my hand. They had a job to do, and they were going to get it done. I thought, "Yes!" And I was part of it. They told me the way it was going to be, and I liked that. I didn't want to have to second-guess them. If they had something to tell me, I wanted to hear it straight. And that is the way they worked with me. I didn't have to be on guard; I could relax because I trusted that they would tell me the truth.

Another big help came from family. One of my sisters, Marnin, and her husband took turns taking me to chemotherapy. They really wanted to do it and it freed up Sharon's time. This time I had chemo every two weeks for eleven and a half months. It was a bit of a grind, but I think my brother-in-law, who took me most of the time, actually enjoyed our time together. And I got to know him differently. It was like being introduced to a new person. We would talk about anything and everything; we would try to be light on politics. And I grew closer to my sister. She was very kind. She is also an unbelievable seamstress. She made a special cloth cover for the pressurized chemo bottle. The bag had a strap that would fit over my shoulder so that I could carry it easily. I could then go home. The bottle gave a continuous dose of chemo, and a nurse would come to the house to disconnect it when it was empty. This process gave me so much more freedom. It was always better when I could be home!

Marnin, her husband, and I spent a lot of time together, and during that time they got to listen to me talk. It was quite funny actually. I was on a fairly good dose of steroids, and because of the steroids I became a sort of "Chatty Liz," a little "wired for sound" after chemotherapy, if you will. Talk, talk, talk. But they didn't seem to mind and, spending that time with them was really good. I was grateful for their help and their kindness. Just a little side note: my sister made approximately twenty-five of these cloth chemotherapy bottle covers and donated them to the cancer centre.

In the beginning I thought, "I'm tough, I can do this by myself"— drive to chemo and back. No problem. But it just doesn't work out that way. Having cancer is a humbling experience. I used to talk about this with my brother-in-law. I would get to the clinic for my chemo, and I would see the same people. Then I wouldn't see them because they died. On two or three occasions I said to him, "I feel really shitty about this. I am practically dancing in here—I don't like having the treatment and I don't like what it is doing to my body, but I feel guilty because I am doing better than a whole bunch of people in this room." Thirty percent of the people in the room looked like they were already dead. I found that hard to take, and my brother-in-law told me he found it difficult at times too.

And even though I was better off than some of the people in the clinic, I kept feeling sick. I really wanted to know when or if I was ever going to feel better. I felt shitty all the time and I kept thinking, wondering, "Is this the new normal or what?" I wasn't ready to die but I did think about my mortality from time to time.

I did have a break for about a year, and I was feeling pretty good. I was working a bit, enjoying my life. I was still getting checked, but the doctors didn't see anything of concern. I still had cancer in my body, but it was under control. But then in April 2020 the cancer was back. I had a routine CAT scan and it showed new growth. I was angry that I was going to put Sharon through this again. I was going to be laid up again, and Sharon was going to have to take care of me. Again. I turned to Sharon at one point and said, "Here we go again." Shit.

There were new tumours in my lung and the doctors decided to use radiation. I had twenty radiation treatments. They prepped me a couple of weeks in advance of the treatments and told me what would happen. The doctor did all the necessary measurements and the tattoos for where the radiation would go. My brother-in-law came with me for the first radiation treatment because I had no idea how I was going to feel after the treatment, if I was going to be okay afterwards. And to be honest with you, I was nervous. I told him after that I was glad he came. When they turned on the machine and the action started, I wasn't sure how I would be, so having him close by was good. In the end, I was fine, and I drove myself to the rest of the appointments. Thankfully I was able to drive myself because the world was now battling a pandemic. COVID19 had arrived and that meant no one could come in with me anyway. The hospital was so quiet; no one was allowed in unless they absolutely had to be there. And I still received great support from the medical team even in the midst of the pandemic.

In the midst of the radiation therapy, I had to have a procedure on my liver. I had a tumour there and the doctors wanted to deal with it directly. I took a Tuesday off from radiation and had the liver procedure done the next day, on Wednesday. I thought I might be able to do both sessions but, in the end, decided I wouldn't try it. It turned out to be a good decision. There's no way I could have done both the same day.

The first thing they did in preparation for the liver procedure was to pump three litres of fluid into my abdomen to protect my organs from the effects of the test. Then they put these plastic plates right by my solar plexus and screwed them down. That restricts your chest movement so they can get accurate measurements for the test. The technician said, "I don't know why this isn't fitting nicely." I laughed and said, "Well, I can tell you why—I look like I'm pregnant." So much fluid! They carried on with the test. The procedure took approximately two hours. The interventional radiologist inserted a long probe through my abdomen to a tumour in my liver and microwaved it. This procedure is called radio frequency ablation and it was used to break up the tumour. And the next day I was back having radiation. I was a little sore, but I went anyway. Finally I finished my radiation in July 2020. My energy level was probably 80 or 85 percent, but it had taken me a bit to get over the liver test. I still have a cough, more of a tickle really, as a result of the radiation. I'm scheduled to go back in four to six weeks for a CAT scan, and those results will tell the doctors if there is anything new going on that they need to pay attention to. It's the waiting game, always the waiting game. Never easy.

It is always in the back of my mind—I have stage 4 colorectal cancer. There are metastases and the doctors have said, "We are going to have to keep an eye on it." My thoughts are, "I really want you to keep an eye on it. I will be very compliant." And I am hoping that if it pops up, it will be some place where we can deal with it. If it pops up in my brain, I won't be too pleased because they probably won't be able to do anything. But there are so many things that medicine can do. As the radiation oncologist said to me, "If this was fifteen to twenty years ago, you would be dead. We didn't do this stuff then." The radiation procedure I had has only been around for about seven years. The machines and the technology just weren't there yet. Even since Sharon's treatment, things have changed so much. I think the more technology, the better. I believe it can help with my longevity. But there must be a limit to how much radiation treatment I can handle. I think of all the CAT scans I have had. So many X-rays! I don't want to have to go through it again, but if I have to, I will. And I am hoping for a break—maybe a long one. I love life and I have a beautiful wife, children, and grandkids that keep me going.

Having cancer changed the way I looked at life. I live every day now like it is my last. I don't want to say that I am more adventurous or anything like that. But I really think it's neat getting up in the morning. When my feet hit the carpet, I think, "Jesus, you know, this is really nice!" I would never have thought of that before. I try not to sweat the small stuff. Now, when the day comes, I think, "Fantastic!"

I got through all the surgeries and treatments—that was a bit of a surprise. Before each surgery I wondered if I would wake up. I had a heart attack years before, and I worried that the pre-existing condition would impact this new situation. But so far so good. I'm not saying that I'm unscathed, but I did actually get through it. At times it is hard not to feel sorry for yourself. I have felt sorry for myself when I think of my own mortality. Is my time up? These thoughts can stick in the back of my mind. The images of patients at the cancer centre that are a lot worse off than me help remind me that, for now, I am okay. And in spite of the burden I feel I have been for Sharon, I'm still married!

Hindsight is interesting. If I was doing parts of life over, I would have had more regular checkups. For example, I had a colonoscopy ten years before this last one. It would have been good to have it sooner. I quit smoking in 1996, and I quit because I had a heart attack. Perhaps I could have drank a little less. Overall, I would have treated myself a little better, taken better care of my health. And another message—remember to love yourself. It isn't easy to do but it is important. Whatever that means to you, do it.

One of the things I would offer to others is, don't give up. I truly believe we have the power within ourselves to heal ourselves. And at the same time, don't be afraid to ask your health care providers the hard questions. Don't sit back, don't be complacent. Try to have the attitude that says, "We have a problem here, let's get it fixed." It is also really helpful to have an advocate. It doesn't have to be a family member, but it does have to be someone you trust, someone who can support you and can share their wisdom with you. No matter what is wrong with you, it's very hard to navigate the health care system. It is so complex. Having someone with me, someone in my corner, made all the difference. I was very lucky. My sister Marnin is the health care advocate for our family. She is just a great resource. She would ask questions or help me ask questions. Sharon is also a great advocate for my care and interests, and she can really think outside the box. She is very reassuring when I become anxious. My children, Clare and Eric, always know the right time to call and ask about how the treatment is going and offer to help in any way they can. And the grandchildren—well, they just constantly warm my heart.

And be cautious about what you read. I would look at my medical reports online because it was fun. I would read them and look up some of the big words. But then I would see a definition for a word and think, "Fuck—that doesn't sound very good!" You need to be really careful about using "Dr. Google"—you can really scare yourself!

People's reactions to my illness were very interesting. I went to a few social gatherings alone after my diagnosis. They were generally police retirement parties, and most people had heard that I had cancer. Some people had absolutely no problem talking to me. They were very empathetic and supportive in any way they could be. Other people didn't talk to me, couldn't talk to me, because they just didn't seem to know what to say. It was as if they were gobsmacked—they didn't know what the hell to do with me. It was like they wished they didn't have to see me. It was very uncomfortable. Here we had worked together for over thirty-five years, and suddenly they were tongue-tied. It may be human nature, I don't know, but it sure made me feel weird.

Gestures of kindness always surprised me, and they came from unexpected places. Our neighbours would ask Sharon about me, and that always made me feel good. They aren't close friends, but they cared enough to check on me. Or if they saw me out, they would stop to talk. I wouldn't give them a big diatribe about what was going on with my treatment, but it was really nice to know they cared enough to check in. It never failed to make me feel good. My wife's friends did all sorts of stuff. They would let the dogs out if we weren't home. They brought meals over—many acts of simple kindness. It was really nice. My son's father-in-law offered this fall to come and help clean up the gardens. He was concerned that I might not be feeling up to it. This man is six or seven years older than me, but he was concerned and ready to help. Sharon kept a private Facebook group that would update friends. This helped a lot because at times I didn't feel like talking to people on the phone. It was hard to accept the kindness at first, but it got easier with time because they genuinely wanted to help. And I was surprised by the people who should have checked in, people I expected to check in, and didn't.

One of the biggest questions in all of this is about *resilience*. I hadn't really thought much about it until now, but I think resilience is the ability to bounce back and come back hard and determined to change the outcome. I know you can't always change the outcome, but you can figure out how to act and react to the situation. I firmly, firmly believe that my resilience came from my mother. She taught me what it meant to be resilient. My mother really wore the pants in the family. She preached toughness to my six sisters because they were women. She believed they had to be better than men to get ahead. She preached and preached, saying, "You have to be tough. When the chips are down, you've got to keep on plugging, plugging on." She believed there were certain tools we all had to have, and the biggest one was education. If we wanted further education, no matter what it was for, the cost was covered. My father made sure we had summer jobs to earn our spending money, but my mother took care of tuition and anything else it took for us to get an education.

I was the only one of eight kids that didn't take her advice, at least right away, but the others did, and it worked out well. I took a different route. I left school at sixteen and worked and eventually attended an adult education program to obtain a GED (grade 12 equivalency certificate). This made me eligible for community college, where I obtained a diploma as a registered nursing assistant. Eventually I joined the Toronto Police and remained there until I retired.

My mother had cancer. She never complained. When she was staying in Toronto with my sister Marnin during her treatments, my police supervisor would say to me, "Take one of the unmarked cars and take your mom to chemotherapy." My mother was tough, very, very resilient, and I owe a lot of my toughness to her. She led by example. She didn't get married until she was thirty-two years of age; she had ten pregnancies and eight kids. She smoked a couple packs of cigarettes a day. She was tough!

And then there is Sharon. My wife. She has had a tremendous effect on me. We have been together since we were eighteen years old. I have always loved her, but throughout this time I have come to appreciate her so much more. She has put up with so much crap—all the shift work, overtime, and all the health challenges. And she has done so much for me. I believe that someone can love you but that doesn't mean they will *do* anything for you. They aren't going to go the extra mile for you. But Sharon has gone that extra mile over and over. I believe she's probably a lot tougher than I am but in a different way. She is very encouraging and believes that we can both get through these health challenges. I told her recently that if she still had the bill from when she got me, I would be going back! Luckily, the return date has expired.

This cancer journey isn't over. I still have tumours in my lungs, and I am not sure what will happen next. At times I daydream that cancer didn't happen, that there weren't any surgeries. It would be nice if everything was peaches and cream. Then reality sets in and the journey continues.

And I said it before, but it is really important—don't forget to love yourself. Sometimes over the last four years, when I reflected on what was happening to my body and my mind, I wanted to take the time to do things just for me, little things. At times I wanted to be the only one that I had to care for or worry about, just for a little while. But even thinking about it made me feel selfish. Looking back, I know it wasn't selfishness; it was me taking care of me, remembering to love myself.

Complicated but important.

And as I wait for yet another set of tests, I think, like I always do, "Let's get 'er done." My mother used to say this, and my son likes to say it. It's our family rallying call—we can do this!

Kim's Reflection

Cancer continues to plague Paul. Just when he thought it was over, it came back. And then it came back again. As I write this reflection, he waits for the phone to ring. But in spite of the waiting, he continues to live as he always has. His days are full. I can close my eyes and see him riding his lawn mower; I see him leaning against the kitchen counter with a beer in his hand. I see him gently stroke the head of one of his dogs. Cancer looms in his mind and it slips into mine as well. But his humour and grace outshine the fear.

Frankl talked extensively about the importance of facing the reality of your situation and Paul did just that. There wasn't a moment when he didn't face his circumstances. He made it clear to his doctors that he wanted them to be honest with him so that he could manage his illness. He accepted nothing but the truth. Stockdale's paradox as defined by Jim Collins was Paul's next step—accepting the current situation and believing or imagining a better future. Paul always looked forward. And he keeps looking forward. It isn't easy, but he has hope. To be hopeful in the midst of dire circumstances is the bedrock of Frankl and Stockdale's work.

Frankl's book is called Man's Search for Meaning because he believed that when life holds no meaning, there is no hope. And Paul understood that, he understood how critical it was to find meaning in this altered existence. He worked whenever he was well enough. He kept doing his chores. And most importantly, he reached out to his wife and children in new ways because he needed their support.

Paul never doubted the seriousness of his situation but finding moments when he could laugh eased the fear that would settle in unexpectedly. Throughout our interview, there were moments punctuated by laughter. Even when Paul talked about poignant moments in the cancer unit, surrounded by very ill people, he still found things to chuckle about, like the day he realized that he wouldn't have to face hair loss. Although debilitating treatment would cause him great discomfort, Paul said he would be okay because, well, he was already bald! His sense of humour helped him maintain perspective.

Paul's story took me to a different area of the literature. Humour is a theme underpinning Paul's attitude. He laughs like no one else I know. Dr. Heather Lonczak wrote, "Humor just feels good; it distracts us from our problems and promotes a lighter perspective."5 She goes on to talk about the studies that describe humour as a strength. That is one of Paul's strengths, his superpower. His willingness to laugh about the silly things that were happening helped him and those around him manage the difficult parts. As the great humorist Mark Twain reminded us, "The human race has one really effective weapon, and that is laughter."

Paul's sense of humour has not, for one moment, minimized his understanding of the seriousness of the situation. But like Frankl, Stockdale, and

---

5   Heather Lonczak, "Humor in Psychology: Coping and Laughing Your Woes Away," blog post on Positive Psychology.com website, January 28, 2021, https://positivepsychology.com/humor-psychology/.

many others, he believes that life holds meaning until there is no more life. Frankl said, "Humour was another of the soul's weapons in the fight for self-preservation" (p. 43). It is a fundamental aspect of resilience. With a chuckle, Paul said, "I really think it's neat getting up in the morning. When my feet hit the carpet, I think, 'This is really nice.'"

As I drew close to the end of Paul's interview, I asked him if he had a favourite poem or song. He sent me a short list of musicians. Nothing else—no comments, no additional direction. I read through the lyrics for every song by each artist. Twice. There were a lot of lyrics! Finally I found the words I was looking for in Mark Knopfler's song "Why Worry." Knopfler reminds us that good things can happen after bad things and sometimes it is good to let worry rest. That captures Paul's spirit for me.

Sharon and Paul

Sharon was diagnosed with cancer in September 2011. She underwent treatment for the next few years. Just as she was emerging from the treatments in 2015, Paul had a terrible fall. He severely damaged his knee, landing him in an extensive recovery program. Sharon needed to shift away from her own recovery process and concentrate on Paul. They got through that ordeal, and just when they thought they were in the clear, Paul was diagnosed with cancer. It was 2016. Once again, they were tossed into a world filled with doctors, tests, chemotherapy, and radiation. Paul continues to live with recurring bouts of cancer.

I interviewed them separately for the first part of the chapter and then I interviewed them together to ask how they cared for each other, what they learned about themselves, and how their own resilience helped them stay the course in the face of ongoing distress.

Kim: Sharon, how did your cancer experience impact how you cared for Paul?

Sharon: When Paul was diagnosed with cancer, we had already been through almost a year dealing with his knee and, to be honest, I was tired. I was with him during that first round of surgery and chemo, but when the cancer came back eighteen months later and it became clear that treatment was going to be indefinite, I thought, "I can't do this."

There was a limit to what I could do because I still needed to take care of myself while I cared for Paul. It all felt like too much. So I was happy to have his sister and brother-in-law take him to the next rounds of chemo. They were happy to help. It was a real bonus for me. It gave me a break. When I went with Paul for the first round of chemo it was such a reminder of everything I had gone through, and it felt like I was being traumatized again. When Paul started the second round it was good for him and for me that he had other people with him who had a different experience with the process. Having his sister step in helped me put some boundaries around what I would and wouldn't do for Paul. There were so many reminders of my own experience with the health system, not all of them good.

Kim: Paul, how did caring for Sharon impact or inform your ongoing experience with cancer?

Paul: There were times after my diagnosis when I felt sorry for myself, but I had witnessed Sharon going through chemo, and she had been so sick. I had issues during chemo, and I was sick, but nothing like what Sharon went through. I don't know how she did it. There were times that felt touch and go. Sharon is an exceptionally strong person, but she was so sick. I thought to myself, "I hope I don't get that sick, I don't want to be where she was." I have thought about how lucky I have been because I've never been as sick as Sharon was. During the first round of my chemo, Sharon went above and beyond the call of duty. When I started the second round of chemo, my sister and brother-in-law stepped in to help, and they continue to help. I have tests coming up and they will take me. It makes me feel good to know that Sharon doesn't have to take me. She is there when I get home, but for a little while she is free from having to care for me.

Kim: Sharon, how did your own resilience help you care for Paul?

Sharon: Resilience ebbs and flows. I keep working on being resilient, and one of the ways I do that is remembering to be kind to myself, to do the inner work that keeps me grounded. And doing that makes supporting Paul easier. Right now, Paul doesn't need physical help, but there are times when emotional support is needed. For example, the doctor called the other day and said that Paul has a cyst in his rectum. Paul immediately decided it must be cancer, and I said to him, "You need to not go there, not until you have to." I reminded him that all our days are numbered—it doesn't matter who you are—so we need to enjoy each day. I try to be present with him, with everyone, every day. It doesn't always work out that way but most of the time it does. So as long as I keep working on myself, Paul gets the benefit. I have learned that resilience isn't about going back to the way things were. Resilience is about learning and moving forward one step at a time, living one moment at a time, and trusting in the uncertainty.

Kim: Paul, how did your own resilience help you care for Sharon?

Paul: My resilience comes from the past, my upbringing, my childhood, and the influence of my mother. But it was hard to be resilient when Sharon was so sick. It was very taxing, and I knew that I had to suck it up. This wasn't going to go away anytime soon, and I wanted to be strong for Sharon. She needed my help, and I didn't want to let her down.

And all the way along, I believed there was light at the end of the tunnel. Sharon was and is very strong and tenacious, and I believed that because of that, she would make it through. That made me want to try even harder to make sure I didn't fall apart.

Kim: How do you take care of yourself—your soul?

Sharon: On the hard days, a bit of laughter helps. And being outside, walking the dogs. It is hard to describe, but when I come back from my walks, I am okay. Everything is good. I have always known that being in nature was good for me, but it wasn't as explicit as it is now. I am not sure I understood why I loved it, but now I do.

Paul: One thing that I love is being on my lawn tractor. I play music and I just tune out. Sharon goes for walks, and when she comes back, she is like a different person. She is one with nature and now she knows it. I didn't know that I loved being outside. Now I understand how much I love the big space. I enjoy watching the birds and feeding them. We have so many species, and I find watching them so relaxing.

Kim: What insights or surprises have you had about each other's resilience?

Sharon: Sometimes I am surprised by Paul's perseverance through all that he has gone through. Most of the time he takes life one day at a time—not always, but a lot of the time. Of course, he worries about things, and that is fair. It has been a long journey and cancer isn't going away until he dies. But I see him enjoying the smaller things around him that he never really paid attention to before. He has learned to appreciate the moments.

Paul: Sharon gives herself totally; she is not selfish. She may be in pain herself, but she is still thinking about me. Or of someone else who needs her attention. She has always been resilient, but she is even more so now. And she reminds me that focusing on the "what ifs" isn't helpful. It is nice to have someone who keeps me on track.

Kim: You both have a wonderful sense of humour. Did humour help? How?

Sharon: Humour is important. It can lighten the mood, and that helps keep perspective. It helps us focus on what *is* versus what might be when we can't do more than what we are doing. We can either be happy here in this moment or we can crawl into our dark holes. Of course, there are times when we need to go to the dark place. It is okay. Laughter helps us see the light. In those humorous moments we can take a breath and renew our spirits. When in those moments of laughter, everything else falls away and you are free.

Paul: I don't think I am purposely funny, but at times it just comes out. When I laugh, I am in a better place. It can take me away from a difficult situation. And I would rather feel happy instead of shitty.

Kim: Has your relationship changed?

Sharon: The reality that Paul might be gone, or I might be gone, is always right there. There is quiet tension around the three-month check-ups. We wait to hear the latest news—how much more time do we have? What do they want to do now? Even when it is good news, the tension is there while we wait to hear. The last year has been good because Paul's tumours haven't changed too much, but we know that can change quickly. There is stress for sure. And we are making the best of it.

Paul: There are changes. Whether we show it or not, there is more stress at times. I am always waiting to hear news about something, whether it is good or bad. Sharon will be waiting too. I think we have a strong relationship, and all this sickness has put a strain on it from time to time.

Kim: Often, when we look back on a traumatic time, there have in fact been small gifts that emerge. Have you received any such gifts?

Paul: This journey has made me much more self-aware. The greatest gift I have received is Sharon's loving care throughout my illness. It is a gift and a blessing that we are both still here, cohabitating. We haven't killed each other!

Sharon: My enduring resilience. I didn't know how deep my resilience went until I needed it. Without my own resilience I wouldn't have been strong enough to go through my cancer and then be with Paul while he continues to go through his.

Kim: Final thoughts?

Sharon: I don't think there are final thoughts, not until it is time to cross to the other side. It is a journey, and hopefully we will both know ourselves fully when that time arrives.

Kim's Reflection

I was surprised by how difficult it was to interview Sharon and Paul together. I realized after the fact that I felt like I was intruding, as if I had taken one step too many into their private world. They were generous with their time, and thoughtful in their responses. They reviewed the transcripts, clarified ambiguous points, and added a few additional thoughts. Yet it felt like there were words unspoken. I wanted to push a little harder, just in case that one extra question elicited an unspoken gem.

Then I caught myself. Sharon and Paul had given me all I asked for and all I needed. With compassion, humour, and grace, they had told me how they are making their way through a world not of their choosing, but the one they have, nonetheless, been given. They take care of each other, sometimes by stepping in to help and sometimes by getting out of the way. Gifts to each other.

CHAPTER FIVE: LIZ

Kim's Story

I MET LIZ IN 1988. *We both worked in health care, doing similar work but in different organizations. We worked on projects together, travelled together for conferences, and found plenty of time to sip wine and discuss all the issues of life. She was funny, kind, irreverent, and really smart. We became good friends, and that friendship has endured for over thirty years.*

She was married to Daniel, a lovely man, who terrified me the first time I met him. Liz and I were sitting in a hotel bar, having a glass of wine, and catching up on all the hospital gossip. The bar wasn't in the best part of town, so from time to time, rather unsavoury characters would wander through. As we sat talking, I saw one of these fellows heading our way. He was large and somewhat scruffy. I leaned toward Liz and quietly said, "There is a scary-looking fellow coming our way. Just keep talking and I will keep an eye on him." Well, instead of doing what I asked, she immediately turned to see who I was looking at. And instead of pretending to ignore him, she jumped up, gave him a huge hug, turned back to me, and, laughing, said, "Kim, this is Daniel."

They were a happy, easygoing couple who shared everything. They were kind to each other, and laughter filled their house. They bantered back and forth all the time about house repairs. Daniel liked to take his time with those repairs and it drove Liz a little crazy. They had matching recliner chairs for watching TV, they loved camping and travel. They just fit.

And then one day it was over.

Liz's Story:

Sunday, December 19, 1999—I remember the day very clearly. We had moved into a new home in September and were still getting settled. We loved this new house. It was brand new, very modern, with heated concrete floors and a beautiful kitchen in the middle of the open-plan main floor. Daniel was thrilled to finally have the space to create a proper workshop using the two-car garage. I was thrilled to be in a brand-new place after living for ten years in an old character home that was always in a state of mini-renovations. Daniel was doing his usual "Daniel" thing, running around making a coffee table and end tables for me. He loved woodworking and over the years he had made stools, bowls, pieces of furniture, Christmas decorations and toys for our nieces and nephews.

Daniel had just started a new position at WorkSafeBC, and the new role required travelling to other places in BC. He had been away for a couple of weeks and was glad to be home, working on the coffee table project. He had spread his project out in the basement, ready for varnishing. I was upstairs doing housework, happy to have him back. We were enjoying our new house, and in many respects, it was a typical day for us—a normal, relaxing, rainy, inside Sunday. He did tell me later in the evening that he wasn't feeling well—vague symptoms. We both assumed it was from breathing in the fumes from the varnish.

Monday, December 20—Early that morning, Daniel said he wasn't feeling well. That wasn't unusual because he had a terrible time with kidney stones. But he seemed strangely worse than usual, so I thought, "You know what, I'm going to take the day off work." I didn't usually do that when he was feeling unwell, but for whatever reason, I did that day. Something about him that day must have made me think this was more serious. I actually phoned our family doctor, who often helped us out when Daniel was having one of his numerous kidney stone attacks. He would usually call the emergency department (ED) and let them know we were coming so we didn't need to wait so long for pain relief. But on this day, he didn't know how to diagnose Daniel's vague symptoms and suggested keeping an eye on him and taking him to the ED if he felt worse.

I was doing that kind of "wifey" thing of getting him tea and coffee. He spent the day sitting downstairs in a recliner watching TV. Around 5 p.m. he called out to me in this strange way; it was very odd. I was upstairs doing something, and I ran downstairs. He said, "I feel really bad. There's something wrong with me." Then he got up to go to the bathroom and he just walked straight into a wall and fell over, flat on his back. I thought he had died. I ran over to him and he was just lying there. He was still conscious, and I tried to pick his head up. I said, "Oh my God, what happened?" He didn't say anything. I wasn't usually very good in crisis situations, but I just knew that this was really bad, so I ran to the phone and dialled 911. I had no idea what was going on, but I knew there was something bad about this situation. Something was very wrong with Daniel.

The first responders from the fire department arrived. Just at that moment my sister Dee phoned me to discuss Christmas plans. My parents were going to spend Christmas with my sister Laura in Nanaimo. Daniel and I were going to spend Christmas Day with Dee and her family. I told Dee quickly that I couldn't talk because the fire department was here and would likely be taking Daniel to the ED. Then I hung up and went back to Daniel's side. The firefighters tried to get him to sit up, but he kept passing out. The ambulance arrived next and, realizing that something weird was going on, whisked him off to the hospital. The firefighters had to carry him out to the ambulance, which was very difficult because he was a big man. I followed in my car and met him in the emergency department.

When I arrived, I asked where he was, and they said something like "Ah, yes, the patient with cardiac/heart issues." That was the first time anyone had mentioned heart problems. When I found him, the doctor told me he thought it was something to do with Daniel's heart, but at that point they really had no idea what was happening. I sat for hours by his bed, waiting to find out what was going on. At one point all the monitors started beeping and it looked to me as if Daniel had died. I ran out to get help and they came running. The nurse said he was bleeding internally but they didn't know from where. And they needed to stop it. She said that it had taken time to get a surgeon (it was Christmastime and every-one was away) and an OR, but now they were ready to go. At that point they just wheeled him away for surgery.

I had been in the ED with Daniel so many times with kidney stones and other bizarre ailments. So being there again was, in a weird way, just another visit. I knew this was serious, but I really believed that they would fix whatever was wrong and we would be on our way. Finally, at about midnight, a social worker came up to me and said, "Isn't there somebody you can call?' I am sure she was thinking, "Does this person have no family?" And at that point I realized that this situation was really bad. Daniel had been admitted, they were operating on him, and I was sitting there alone. I was very frightened, very confused.

I phoned my sister Dee and she came right away. Dee was a saint that night. She had four children under the age of ten and lived in North Vancouver. But she didn't miss a beat; she jumped into her car and drove straight to Vancouver General Hospital (VGH). We didn't want to worry my mother and father in the middle of the night, so we didn't call anybody else in the family.

That was one of the most awful nights of my life. They showed Dee and me to the family waiting room for surgery patients. It was a new area, nicely decorated in pale pink colours. But it was also empty, impersonal, claustrophobic, and "cold." Nobody came to talk to us for hours. At some point we decided to go for a walk just to try to ease the rising anxiety and panic that we were both feeling. I remember thinking, "Daniel might die in this operation." None of the health professionals had indicated this— but I just knew it.

It was the week before Christmas and there was no one around, espe-cially at midnight. There were Christmas trees everywhere. We wandered around looking at the Christmas trees. Waiting. We waited for hours and hours because the operation took hours. Finally the surgeon came out, and it was another one of those odd moments because he seemed some-what elated—the surgical team were really impressed with themselves for saving Daniel's life. The doctor said, "It was touch and go there for a while, but we removed a section of his bowel because we think that's where the bleeding was coming from." He went on to say they almost lost him a couple of times during the surgery, and they were pretty happy that he had survived. I was so relieved and thought, "Great, maybe the worst is over." With Daniel out of surgery and in recovery, both Dee and I headed home. It was early Tuesday morning.

Tuesday, December 21—I went back to the hospital later in the morning. I could see by the looks on the doctors' faces that Daniel was not out of the woods yet, that things were not good. They were very careful not to say too much to me. In fact, it was the look on their faces and the lack of information provided me that made me think this was very serious. They never told me what they thought it could be. They did think the surgery the night before had fixed the bleeding, but it hadn't. Daniel was still bleeding. They called in a heart specialist because they were hearing something in his heart that wasn't quite right.

Daniel was in the Intensive Care Unit (ICU) at this point. It was such an awful day, but as awful as it was for Daniel and for me, he was still making me laugh. He could always make me laugh, and this day was no different. He was supposed to be lying on his side and he said to me, "If they want me on my side, they need duct tape. They need to tape me where they want me to be." And all I could do was laugh. There he was in ICU, hardly functioning, and still he was making these stupid jokes. He was never the best patient in the world, but he was always funny.

Wednesday, December 22—They moved him to a regular room. Because of the bowel surgery, Daniel would need to have a colostomy bag. Fine. We didn't need to learn all the ins and outs of it in that moment. But there was a very determined nurse on the unit, and she made it her mission to try to teach us everything we might need to know. Finally Daniel said, "I can't listen to this." It was way too early for any of this information, and they still didn't really know what was wrong with him. Something was still bothering the doctors. They were checking on him very regularly but not saying anything to me.

By Thursday, December 23, Daniel was actually looking a little better. I spent most of the day with him and then, when his sister came, I went home.

My parents were living at Walloper Lake, a small community about 320 kilometres from Vancouver. They had come down to Vancouver and were staying with my sister Samantha for a few days before heading over to Nanaimo for Christmas with my sister Laura. But they changed their plans on the Tuesday and came to stay with me instead. They were with me when my phone rang on Friday morning, December 24.

I was having a shower when the phone rang. Mum answered and brought it to me. "Quick, quick," she said. "It's the hospital."

I got out of the shower—I can still see myself standing in my bedroom, sopping wet with a towel wrapped around me. The doctor said, "I'm really sorry, but your husband has died." I wasn't expecting that at all. I probably should have been because I knew Daniel was very sick, but the doctors weren't expecting it either. It caught everybody off guard.

From that minute my world changed. Completely. I couldn't believe what they were telling me, and yet I knew it to be true. I didn't want to believe. I just didn't want to believe.

I usually have a terrible memory, but for this I remember every moment. I was so grateful that my mum and dad were with me. The hospital needed someone to come and do whatever paperwork was required. But I didn't want to see Daniel. I didn't want to see him dead. I couldn't cope with that. My dear dad went and took care of everything at the hospital.

I couldn't cope with anything. It was like I was catatonic. I could hardly move—I couldn't eat; I couldn't drink; I couldn't do anything except cry. I could not believe Daniel was dead. I was forty-one years old and I had had a pretty sheltered life up until that day, a charmed life. I had never experienced any kind of tragedy. Let's be clear—I had a perfect, happy little childhood. I had my lovely parents and my lovely sisters. My grandmother died, but you expect that to happen. Nothing like this had ever happened to me. No tragedy. Tragedies happened to other people, but not to me. This wasn't part of my story. This was not how things were meant to go. And so I just couldn't go to the hospital. I was such a chicken. The doctors asked for permission to do an autopsy because they wanted to know what had happened, and I said yes. It was all just so awful.

And it was still Christmas Eve. It was a blur of family arriving. My poor mother and father had to call all of Daniel's friends and family.

Making those phone calls must have been so hard—telling people that forty-five-year-old Daniel, healthy, strong, large-as-life Daniel, had suddenly died. Out of the blue.

I remember just sitting on my couch with someone from my family by my side, hugging me, all day. That night I was too frightened to sleep in my bed alone. My sweet mother slept in bed with me. For the next few days, maybe weeks, I slept in a cot downstairs near the spare bedroom that my mum and dad were sleeping in. I just couldn't sleep in "our bed."

I also remember taking down our Christmas tree with all its beautiful, blue-themed decorations. So painful. I couldn't bear to see all these happy Christmas things around me. And to this day, Christmas is a very difficult time of the year for me.

The next day was Christmas Day. December 25, 1999. Mum and Dad were supposed to go to visit my sister Laura for the holidays, but she and her two daughters came to us instead. My sister Dee had four little kids, so no matter what, Christmas had to happen for them. Mum and Dad bundled me into the car, and we went off to Dee's to celebrate Christmas.

When I look back, I was just going through the motions of walking and talking and getting dressed. I know that because all I really felt was this excruciating pain. I remember thinking to myself, "All those things people talk about when other people die—that you have a broken heart. It is true." My heart, my actual heart, felt like it was broken. You see women on the TV that wail and scream and throw themselves onto the ground when they experience tragedy. I wanted to do that. I wanted to scream. I was so angry, and the pain was so deep. I can't describe the pain. It was physical as well as mental and emotional. It was that full range of every horrible emotion you can think of, and they were all raging inside of me.

On top of that pain was the horrible knowledge that this "thing" that happened to me was irreversible. I could not fix it because the only thing that would fix it was Daniel coming back. And he wasn't coming back. It was unfixable. And I didn't know how to deal with this unfixable problem. Every other problem in my life had a solution, there was a way around it. If I just looked at it in a different way, I could figure out a solution. This problem, this situation, this death—this was not fixable. No matter how much I wanted to rewind the tape, I couldn't. There wasn't a different story, there wasn't a different ending. That was the source of the immense pain because that one thing that would make me feel better could never ever happen. It was just so finite. The one thing that I really wanted was Daniel back and that was not possible. I remember sitting on my couch, staring at the floor, and thinking, "It's like someone has taken my life, the one that all fit together before Daniel died, and removed a piece. And every other piece of my life is now just a jumble of disconnected pieces." It's like someone shook up a bag filled with puzzle pieces, all the fragments of my life and threw them on the floor. I didn't know how to put it together because that piece that glued it all together was gone. And it could never come back.

For the first time in my life, I felt emotions that I wasn't familiar with. I was really frightened, and I had never felt fear before. I've never understood fear. I had never had a reason to be frightened. I had a pleasant, lovely little life. But suddenly a really bad thing happened to me and I became very fearful. And I stayed fearful for years after that because now I knew bad things, really bad things, could happen to you. From the first night after Daniel died, I was frightened. I was filled with this childish terror and anger. I wasn't an angry person before Daniel died, but to this day I still feel angry about what happened. It was as if some sort of button was pushed. I felt badly done by and I was particularly angry at God. I couldn't understand why He would take this happy, healthy person. It made no sense. I don't think I will ever fully understand or accept this loss. I have resigned myself to it, but I have never been able to make sense of it and will always wonder how that life with Daniel could have unfolded—should have unfolded.

Traditionally at Christmas our family had this big thing where there were all these presents under the tree, and we handed them out one by one until they were all opened. So we did this on that Christmas Day, like every other year, except it wasn't like all those other years. Daniel was missing. When we were finished, there was this sad little pile of unopened gifts for Daniel. It was unbearable. There were a million and one reminders of what I had lost, and every single thing was like a knife being stuck in my heart.

Unfortunately, Daniel's death caused a huge rift with his family. I know that everybody grieves differently, but his dad and sister were saying and doing things which I found incredibly hurtful. In retrospect, I think they were just hurting too, but their words and actions at the time broke our relationship. I was so brittle and sensitive. You couldn't look at me sideways without me reacting. I was so irrational and unable to have any compassion for anybody else. Looking back, I know it was very selfish, but it was all about *me* at that moment. A day or two after Daniel died, his dad told me he wanted Daniel's truck. It was just a stupid old white Dodge truck, but we had had a ton of fun times in that truck, and asking me for it a day or so after Daniel died—well, it felt wrong.

Then a few days later, his sister said, "My mom gave you a lot of family stuff when you got married, and because you don't have any children, I think it might be better if I had it all back to give to my kids." Twenty years later that makes sense to me but telling me two or three days after my husband died was a reminder not only of his death but also of the only other sadness in my life, which was that we hadn't had kids. It felt like she was telling me that we never sealed our relationship, that our marriage didn't count without children. It was a sudden recognition blood was thicker than water. I was not the bloodline. It hurt so much. I have a lot of regrets about losing touch with Daniel's family, and I wonder if I had stayed in Canada instead of moving away so quickly, I might have been able to mend those relationships. It is too late now but I still think about it.

We had to wait until December 28 to have the funeral so Daniel's dad could travel from Saskatchewan. The waiting was hell. But I got through the funeral. I had no choice. My family and friends carried me through that day. My mother planned the whole funeral with her church connections. Dad took me to a local funeral home to make all the arrangements. I couldn't speak at the service—but my mother helped me write something on my behalf. I don't remember who read it. I do remember one of Daniel's dear friends and work colleagues making a beautiful speech. It was another day in hell.

The first couple of weeks after Daniel died were a blur. I couldn't sleep so I asked the doctor for sleeping pills. He said it must be insomnia and did I really need pills? I said, "You don't understand. Sleep is the only break I get from this constant grief. Pills will let me sleep for the night." Waking up every day was the worst. I would wake up thinking, "Mmm, I am awake and I'm living the nightmare. I don't have nightmares at night. I live a nightmare when I am awake. My every day is now an actual nightmare that I can't wake up from because I am awake." The doctor also suggested antidepressants, but I didn't want them. I had a reason to be depressed. I don't know if I made the right decision. I had worked for many years in palliative care and hospice and, ironically, participated in many grief recovery sessions provided by health care professionals. One of the social workers felt that antidepressant drugs just cover up the inevitable pain and emotions instead of letting you work through them and process your grief. I have since talked to people who have found medication very helpful during a time of grief—so I don't know if I chose the best path for me or not. I do know that I could not have survived without sleeping pills. My horrible routine was to get through the day and knock myself out at night.

Once I stopped taking sleeping pills, I would dream about Daniel. It was a comfort sometimes, but there was sadness too. The dreams left that little glimmer of hope that maybe he didn't die. He never spoke in my dreams, but I knew he was there. I would say, "Why did you go? Why did you do that?" But he never spoke. It was all so depressing. The dreams came and went, reminders that no, he wasn't coming back—this was wishful thinking on my part, just wishful thinking.

My friends were wonderful. I had so much respect for the friends who were brave enough to be part of that circle of grief. My friend Valerie arrived with soup, a great big pot full of soup. She knocked on the door and said, "I won't stay. I just brought food." But she did stay for a few minutes, and my parents' dog, Cleo, sat at my feet while we sat on the couch. I wasn't even thinking about eating but we did need to eat. It was perfect. It was those practical things that helped so much. My friend Gail used to come every day and knock on the door, asking if I wanted to go for a walk. I turned her down at first, and then finally my mum sort of pushed me, saying, "Why don't you go out for a walk?" So I started walking with Gail, and she would just let me talk. She let me go on and on, and that ended up being really helpful. That was the best thing my friends did for me—they listened. The only way I could process what had happened was talking it out. I needed to say everything that I was thinking and feeling out loud. It must have been really hard for people to listen to me, but they did it anyway. I so respected my friends who didn't run a thousand miles from me.

(Kim, I will also be forever grateful for your gentle support during this awful time. That special evening with another friend of yours who had also lost her husband, our trip to La Conner and especially that healing trip to Hong Kong. I remember feeling like I was coming back to life, seeing Hong Kong with you as my special guide. It was truly a turning point in my grief journey.)

I never knew where support would come from. One of those surprises was my boss, Michael. He was a colorectal surgeon and he asked, "Do you want me to walk through the autopsy with you?" I said yes because I couldn't understand the medical jargon in the report. He was amazing. He said, "Look, Liz, I believe that there's a time to live and there is a time to die. Whenever that time—that's when it happens. Daniel had an aortic aneurysm, and he might have had it for a long time; he might have been born with it. It was like a ticking time bomb, and even if we had found it years ago, Daniel would have been faced with a pretty tough decision. To operate or not to operate. Neither choice would have been an easy one. If the doctors had operated on Daniel earlier, there was still less than a 50/50 chance that he would have survived. What you need to know is there is nothing you or Daniel could have done to prevent this from happening."

He was very wise—his words captured exactly what was going through my mind. What could we have done? What should we have done? Did we miss signs? And it was weird because there were signs that something was going on—we just didn't recognize them at the time. Daniel was having all these issues with swallowing, and it's probably because this thing, this aneurysm, was pressing against his esophagus and running down to the heart.

"The other thing you need to know," Michael said, "is that Daniel died really quickly and painlessly." Michael was so professional as he reviewed the autopsy, and it was comforting to listen to the man I thought of as my boss talk to me with such compassion. At the end of the day, the only way I got through those early days and months was because I was carried along by my circle of friends, my family, and people like Michael, who cared for me.

Another time, a woman I didn't even know very well gave me a book called *Seven Choices* by Elizabeth Harper Neeld. The author had a similar experience to mine—her husband died suddenly like Daniel, and they had no children. When I was first given the book, I was angry because I thought, "Choices—are you kidding me? This isn't about choice, there's no choice." I wouldn't even look at it for the longest time; even the title irritated me. But eventually I did read it, and that book became a Bible for me. She wrote her book ten years after her husband died. She kept a journal during those ten years, and then, using her journals and research she had done into grief and loss, defined these seven choices or choice points during the grief process. This was a different approach from the classic ones defined by Kübler-Ross. For example, she talked about how you can choose to live with this pain, the pain of losing someone, for the rest of your life and never rejoin life. And some people do that; the pain from the loss becomes everything. I didn't like her calling it a "choice," but she was right. The choice is not about the thing that happened because you don't have that choice. But you can choose to try to deal with the loss, to figure out how to live with the pain but not allowing the pain to be your whole life.

Reading this book made me think. She'd woven other people's stories into her work as well, and it was comforting to read how other people got through the day, how they approached different situations, and how they moved forward. I was desperate for some sort of manual or cookbook for the bereaved, if you will. How was I supposed to live this new life? It's not something people talk about, and so I wanted this prescription, this outline: What should I do? How could I move on? One day I remember thinking that Daniel would be really upset with me if I just threw my life away in my forties, and I could have done that so easily. But that book—it helped me see that I did have a choice. Stand still or move forward. I could stay in this broken painful state and say, "Poor me; it's so painful and so awful. Why did this happen to me?" Or I could figure out how to take a step forward.

I held myself back in the early days, back from moving forward, from figuring out how to live without Daniel. I railed against the reality so much because I did not want to believe that Daniel was dead, that this had happened to me. It wasn't fair and I didn't want to have to deal with it. I felt cheated and I was angry. I remember thinking, "I wish I could have an actual mental breakdown. Why can't I just have whatever it is that happens to people when they become a mental wreck and end up on a psych ward? Why can't I crawl into a corner and have an actual mental breakdown?" I contemplated suicide in the early days as well. I was driving home from work one day—it was cold and snowy—and I remember thinking, "If I just drove really fast into a brick wall, all of this would end." But there was something deep inside of me that wouldn't let me "quit" or "collapse." Some kind of deep drive that propelled me into surviving and somehow dealing with this loss. And thoughts of my parents and people around me kept me from killing myself too. I couldn't bear to inflict this pain of loss on them. But I did keep wishing that I could retreat into some kind of "mental coma" that would prevent me from feeling and dealing with grief.

I had never understood why people committed suicide because I had never felt a deep enough pain, where I thought that ending my life would be better than living my life. But that was truly an attractive option for me at that point because the pain was unbearable. I couldn't understand how the world kept turning, how life kept going when the world had stopped for me. I was even angry when the daffodils came up in April. Spring was a reminder to me that life was going on for everyone and everything else. It just stood still for me. The world was not mourning— only I was.

Sometimes I think the biggest mistake I made was pushing myself too hard, too fast. I was trying too hard to "get over this." The truth is you never really "get over it." You learn to live with it, and the pain eases, but it never goes away. I should have been kinder to myself, taken the time to process what had happened to me instead of trying to "fix it" somehow and "move on with my life."

I couldn't seem to put my life back together, surrounded by all the memories of Daniel. Even my family seemed to magnify the loss. Being around them, attending family events, was always a reminder of what I had lost. Grief books say you shouldn't make major changes too soon because your ability to make good decisions isn't always balanced. I remember being angry about that idea too, because even if I didn't want it to, my life did have to keep going on because I was alive. I couldn't just sit on a shelf and observe my life, not make any decisions. But like the grief books said, it was really hard for me to make good decisions, so I ran away. It's worked out okay for me in the end, but it made recovery longer.

When I look back on that time, I wouldn't define myself as resilient at all. I looked up the definition of resilience and it said, "Ability to cope with unforeseen circumstances; ability to bounce back quickly." That wasn't me. I don't think I was resilient after Daniel died. I didn't adapt quickly to my new life without him at all. But finally, I went on a mission to put my life back together, a bit of a crazy mission really. And building this new life was easier said than done.

A year after Daniel died, I decided to take a trip by myself for the first time in my life. I spent one week in Mallorca with a friend. It was an amazing healing week, living in a beautiful Spanish villa with my friend. Then one week in London, my birthplace. This was also a kind of healing week as I explored England on a bus tour. But I found it excruciatingly painful ending up each night alone in my hotel room and ordering room service because I couldn't bear to go out alone at night. The third week was spent in Greece. A few days in Athens, a few days in Santorini, and a few days in Mykonos. Greece was a tonic for me. Warm weather, warm people, history. I fell in love with Greece. I met my current husband, Nic, in Mykonos. He was working in the hotel I was staying at. He took me out for dinner, and then we explored the night life in Mykonos. Nic was full of life, optimism, and hope. I wanted my "vacation from life" to go on forever. So after returning from my holiday, I booked a month in Mykonos. Nic and I ended up spending the summer together, exploring Greece and Italy. I will never forget those amazing months. I felt alive again for the first time since Daniel had died. I didn't want it to end. So

I made the decision to move to Cyprus, where Nic was from, and live there for a while. A while turned into twelve years.

Moving to another country was therapeutic at the time because I needed to be away from home. I was in a foreign land with different people. Moving into another relationship so quickly after Daniel had died could have been disastrous. But it wasn't. It was wonderful to be enveloped in Nic's family and truly experience Cypriot culture. In a way, Nic's family was a bit of a replacement family for my family. I learned valuable life lessons about family, and I loved so many things about Cyprus—the weather, the food, the history, the people. In the end, it was very hard to leave Cyprus and all the friends I had made there.

I made a lot of poor decisions along the way, including bad financial decisions. Nic and I tried our hands at a number of businesses. It seemed so exciting and different to me from the staid health care world I had always worked in. However, none of them were very successful, and the losses did have unfortunate consequences on our financial future. But I don't regret trying all those things—each one was an experience. And I can't go back and change any of it. I had this stupid attitude—*just throw caution to the wind*! Daniel and I had always done the *right* thing, the appropriate thing. We saved money, bought a house, and then he died. And I thought, "What's the point of all this? Doing the right thing? I might die tomorrow. I may as well just live with wild abandon and do whatever I feel like." I can see now that I was still grieving, acting out my anger. Unfortunately, this decision to throw caution to the wind was costly in many ways.

In the end, good things came from my decision to run away. Nic was this positive person, and being with him started to make me feel hopeful, feel that maybe I could be happy again. Before I met Nic I wasn't feeling any positive emotions, ever. Day in, day out, nothing but grief. I remember Mum saying, "Your grief is suffocating you." I thought, "Yes, it is, but I don't know how to turn it off. I can't get out of this perpetual cycle of anger, sadness, fear. Grief." There was nothing that made me feel better. And "better" was a stupid word. People would say, "You'll feel better. You'll get over this." Those are ridiculous words that people use. You learn to live with "it" in some weird way, but you don't get over the thing that changes your whole life, that takes away all the happiness you had before "it" happened. I have never really accepted that Daniel died. It's still a source of annoyance to me. I wanted that life very much, the one with Daniel. But it was snatched away. And yet I did find happiness again, and some semblance of normal life, but it was not fast.

I didn't talk to Nic about Daniel often, but when I did, Nic was supportive. He introduced me to a tradition of the Greek Orthodox Church that was very healing. We went together to the church and lit a candle in memory of those who have died. It was a way to remember Daniel. I still do this at Christmas time — it is a way to remember Daniel and other special people in my life who have died. It is a beautiful and comforting ritual.

Our crash-landing back to Canada was another very traumatic experience for me. The economy had completely crashed in Cyprus, and we knew we could never get back on our feet financially there. Canada offered much more opportunity, especially for me. And I really wanted to be back, closer to my parents, particularly to my father, who was battling cancer. I had to restart my life again in my fifties. We had to build from nothing. No jobs, no house, no car. It was exhausting.

It has been seven years since we returned. Looking back, I think, "These last seven years have been an example of my resilience." I didn't cope well when Daniel died, but I have made it through these difficult years. Perhaps that time of loss and grief, that experience, was the foundation that enabled me to cope better with what happened in Cyprus and with our return home. Just the other day I said to Nic, "We've done well, we both got really good jobs. We've managed to buy the apartment. We're very fortunate." When I see what we have accomplished in seven years, I have started to forgive myself for all the bad decisions. I was in a place of deep grief for so long, a place that was foreign to me, and I was so overwhelmed. I had never experienced anything that horrible. Those tough lessons learned over the years have made me better able to deal with whatever comes now. I have more confidence, I trust myself. But it took me a long time. For years and years I was in survival mode, which isn't the best thing. In her book *Seven Choices*, Elizabeth Harper Neeld talks about getting through one day at a time, but unfortunately, that became my life. I thought that if I survived each day, everything was good. The problem is that you stop preparing for the future because you can't imagine that there is a future.

Thinking about resilience takes me back to my parents and how they influenced my life. My mother was always nurturing and comforting. But she is also a fighter and a very strong person. She was the one telling me to pick myself up and get on with life. She pressed me to go back to work after two weeks, and even though it felt like that was too soon, she was right to push me. It is good to have someone who will push, who will say, "Come on, you need to get on with life." She taught me to keep going. And she keeps teaching me with her own actions to this day. I have watched her go through the grief of losing her husband. She was devastated when Dad died and is still having a difficult time adjusting to life without him. But she keeps going.

My dad taught me "how" to go on. He was always a tough but loving father who wanted to coach and mentor his children, help us to navigate life. He didn't say, "Poor you." He would say, "That's life! Hard things have happened, and you need to keep going." Both he and my grandfather lived by a poem written by Rudyard Kipling called "If." Kipling wrote it for his son. It's a really amazing poem and Dad would quote parts of this poem to me at different points in my life, times when things were not going well. Dad continued to quote from this poem in the years after Daniel died, and those words always helped me.

IF
If you can keep your head when all about you
Are losing theirs and blaming it on you,
If you can trust yourself when all men doubt you,
But make allowance for their doubting too;
If you can wait and not be tired by waiting,
Or being lied about, don't deal in lies,
Or being hated, don't give way to hating,
And yet don't look too good, nor talk too wise:

If you can dream—and not make dreams your master;

If you can think—and not make thoughts your aim;
If you can meet with Triumph and Disaster
And treat those two impostors just the same;
If you can bear to hear the truth you've spoken
Twisted by knaves to make a trap for fools,
Or watch the things you gave your life to, broken,
And stoop and build 'em up with worn-out tools:

If you can make one heap of all your winnings
And risk it on one turn of pitch-and-toss,
And lose, and start again at your beginnings
And never breathe a word about your loss;
If you can force your heart and nerve and sinew
To serve your turn long after they are gone,
And so hold on when there is nothing in you
Except the Will which says to them: 'Hold on!'

If you can talk with crowds and keep your virtue,
Or walk with Kings—nor lose the common touch,
If neither foes nor loving friends can hurt you,
If all men count with you, but none too much;
If you can fill the unforgiving minute
With sixty seconds' worth of distance run,
Yours is the Earth and everything that's in it,
And—which is more—you'll be a Man, my son!
Rudyard Kipling

I was so fortunate to have both of my parents. They always really tried to do the right thing for everyone and anyone. And they wanted only the best for their children.

For so long I was afraid, afraid of so many things. I knew I would never have that naïve happiness again I had with Daniel, but I was even afraid to hope for any kind of happiness. What if I was happy and catastrophe struck? I didn't want to have the rug pulled out from under me again. I never wanted to be that hurt again. But I did go on, I did find happiness again. I do find joy again in life in the small things — spending time with family, satisfaction in my job, pride in Nic and me for rebuilding our lives. Resilience is fighting back, making an effort to fight against everything bad that's happened. I feel like I can give myself a little bit of credit for doing what my dad's poem talked about. And I know that even when I doubted myself, I had the seeds of resilience in me. Now they have bloomed. And now I see that I am resilient. It just took time.

Kim's Reflection

Like others in this book, Liz resisted the idea that she was resilient. She didn't see it in herself. It wasn't until we were finished writing this story that she accepted that her strength, her perseverance, defined her as resilient. Participating in this project was very difficult for Liz as she relived so many memories of the loss and pain. But she did it.

One of Frankl's key messages was to accept the current reality of your life and then figure out how to find meaning in that new life. This was very difficult for Liz. Her grief was almost too deep to overcome. Listening to her, I was reminded how both Frankl and Stockdale talked about prisoners who lived with a naïve hope, a belief that life was about to get better, and when it got worse, they died of a broken heart.

For the longest time Liz couldn't see past her broken heart, couldn't figure out how to put the pieces back together. As she said, her life had been a happy magical place with few disruptions. And then Daniel died—a catastrophe of great magnitude. She was ill-equipped for what lay ahead, or so she believed. Liz thought she was broken forever, but somewhere in her she also knew it wasn't okay to do nothing, to stand still. She knew that Daniel would be sad if she let go of the possibilities in front of her. Running away was her first step forward. As distressed as many of her family and friends were, this in fact was when she began to face the harsh reality of Daniel's death. Frankl and Stockard never said there was one way to move, only that to live a full life you had to face your reality. Liz did it her way.

Death of a spouse ranks in the top five most stressful events in a person's life. It was hard to watch Liz stumble through her grief, slipping backwards and sideways. She knew who she used to be; she was Daniel's wife. She forgot for a while that she was also Liz, a competent, strong woman. In her book Seven Choices: Finding Daylight After Loss Shatters Your World, *Elizabeth Harper Neeld said of herself, "It was a time of chaos. My life was liquid—it had no form. I didn't know who I was; I didn't know where I was; I didn't know where I was going. You see, I was defined before" (p. 43). Neeld's words made sense to Liz, so she went to find herself again. She found meaning in her new life with Nic in Cyprus, echoing Frankl's belief that finding new meaning helps reorient you to the future.*

Neeld went on to say, "I have found equilibrium again. I have freedom from the domination of grief. Life now has a 'new normal.' I am not stuck. I am again a participant in the wonderful mystery called life" (p. 5). That is what Liz eventually found, but to get there she had to accept the reality that Daniel was dead. This exemplifies Frankl's idea of meaning making. He talked about the importance of finding a reason to live even in the face of tragedy. Liz resisted, but almost despite herself she gradually began to find new comfort, new possibilities. She fell in love again, giving new purpose to her life.

As Liz talked to me, the notion or metaphor of "slow burn" kept coming to mind. It helped me understand that sometimes people return to life slowly. It doesn't mean they aren't resilient. It means that they need time to adjust, to work through what happened to them. And there is an inner force pushing them onward in small, incremental movements, sometimes in spite of themselves. That was Liz.

Her path back was a turbulent one, but now she has a life where happiness once again resides. This unexpected happiness rekindled Liz's desire to live fully. A surprise to her but not to me. She is my resilient friend, Liz.

CHAPTER SIX: SHAWNA

Kim's Story

UNLIKE THE PREVIOUS STORIES, *which were told to me by my friends, this is a story about my daughter, Shawna, and my grandson, Cameron, so it is also about me. Cameron was diagnosed with a brain tumour in April 2006. He was five years old. Everything changed for us that day. The sky seemed to grow dark, and the world around us was frightening. I felt like I was drowning. But I had to find a way to help, a way to support Shawna, her husband, Jim, and Cameron. In that moment, I didn't know how.*

There is no way to stay neutral when catastrophe hits your family, your child. Even if the child is an adult, you leap to action. I watched Shawna closely over the weeks, months, and years that followed Cameron's diagnosis. I saw her strength when all she saw was weakness; I saw her determination when all she saw was failure. Every step she made was fuelled by a relentless desire to support her son however she could. No matter what happened on any given day, she pushed herself forward. She didn't give up, didn't give in to the despair she felt. How can that not be resilience?

In places, my memories mingle with Shawna's memories. I remember details that got lost for Shawna in the immediacy of the moment. I hope they add clarity and focus to our story.

Shawna's Story:

This story began the first week of April 2006. Cameron had been getting more and more clumsy that week. He was stumbling, bouncing off door frames. At first we thought it was a nervous reaction to something going on at school. He was in kindergarten, and the transition to school had been difficult for him. Cameron was a shy, quiet boy, and new situations made him anxious. When we took him to the doctor, he told us he thought Cameron had an inner ear infection or bubbles in the fluid of the ear canal. But it just kept getting worse.

Finally, my husband, Jim, decided that we should take Cameron to the hospital. We took him to Emergency at BC Children's Hospital on Saturday, April 8, 2006. The emergency doctor checked Cameron over and everything seemed fine until he looked into Cameron's eyes. He could see pressure on the optic nerve. Seeing that pressure on the nerve put everything else into motion. I remember that moment clearly. The doctor told us that he could see some kind of pressure on the optic nerve, and it needed to be checked. I remember nothing else after that until they moved us to a private room in the emergency department, explaining that we would have to stay overnight. They did an X-ray that Saturday afternoon and told us they would do a CAT scan in the morning. Jim and I stayed with Cameron overnight, and in the morning, they did the CAT scan. Then they came back and said they needed to do an MRI. When Cameron came back from the MRI, I cuddled up with him under his comforter. After a little while, probably about an hour, a doctor came in and started to talk. I wasn't listening but I remember that as soon as he began, my mother grabbed the doctor and shoved him out the door. Jim followed her, closing the door behind him. I stayed put and just held on to Cameron. I sang and read to Cameron, anything to distract him and myself from what was going on.

Kim: I realized as soon as the doctor started to talk that he was about to blurt information that, although probably accurate, was going to be delivered to Shawna and Jim in a way that would be very destructive. I learned later that he was a resident on rotation and had never had to deliver potentially life-threatening news to a family about their child. I worked in health care and I had seen doctors give families bad news. Some were kind and compassionate. Some were not. And some, especially inexperienced doctors, were "blurters"—no thought to how their words would impact the family. We had one of those, and even though I knew whatever it was he wanted to tell us was important, I wanted to protect Shawna from his naïve approach.

We then waited for the on-call neurosurgeon to arrive. When he did, he explained to us that Cameron had a tumour pressing on his brain and it had to be removed. He said he wouldn't know exactly what kind of tumour it was until it was removed, but no matter what kind it was, it had to come out. We learned later that the tumour was the cause of Cameron's stumbling, his headaches, and his morning sickness. The doctor went on to say that he would do the surgery the following morning—Monday, April 10. They moved us up to a ward where Cameron, Jim, and I spent the night. I don't remember anything from that night other than holding Cameron and singing to him like I had the night before, like I did every night before he went to bed. Ever since I was a little girl, I could block things that I didn't want to think about, and this was one of those times. My memory of those early days of Cameron's illness is blank.

Kim: The surgeon's name was Ash Singhal. He was amazing. He took Shawna, Jim, Chad (my husband), and me into the backroom behind the nurses' station. There were a number of computers, but only one of the screens was live. There was a picture of Cameron's brain on the screen. Using a pen, he circled the area where the tumour was sitting. I had a hard time seeing the tumour. Dr. Singhal simply pointed, and then I saw it. It was huge, the size of an orange. How could something so big be inside the head of someone so small? He spoke quietly and clearly, stopping for questions along the way. Before he left us, he made sure we understood what he would do in the operation and what we could expect afterwards. It felt like we were in good hands. And yet, I could hardly breathe.

When the nurses took Cameron to the operating room the next morning, only one of us could go all the way into the room with him. I went as far as the doors, and Jim went the rest of the way. As the door closed behind them, I turned, and I hugged my mother. She told me it was going to be okay. I yelled at her and I stamped my foot. I shouted, "No, it is not going to be okay. This is not okay." She hugged me back and said, "You are right, this isn't okay." I slid to the floor and sobbed.

After a few minutes Jim came back through the door. His mother was waiting with us and she reached for Jim. She hugged him and my mother hugged me. The doctor said it would be an eight-hour surgery, so we left the operating room area and went to the Starbucks. April 10—it was a very long day, one of the longest days of my life.

Kim: When we finished our coffees, we went back to the waiting room. Jim's parents and Chad and I sat with Jim and Shawna for the next eight hours. As hour eight passed, I looked out the door. Way down the hall, a figure dressed in surgical scrubs was striding towards us. It was Dr. Singhal, Cameron's doctor, and he was shouting, "It is over; everything is okay." He kept saying those words until he reached us. He hugged Shawna and Jim, smiling at the rest of us. He told us Cameron was in recovery and would be moved to the ICU as soon as he woke up. He told us that as soon as Cameron was settled in ICU, we would be able to see him. In that moment there was no family as happy as we were. Each of us took our turn to thank Dr. Singhal for what he had done.

Cameron was in the ICU for two days and then moved to a ward. On the second day in ICU, the nurse asked Shawna to leave for a few minutes because she had to turn Cameron and she was worried that it would distress Shawna if the movement caused Cameron pain. Then she turned to me and asked if I would stay. After Shawna left, I helped the nurse move Cameron. It is a moment I have never forgotten. As we gently lifted him, his eyes flew open, and he stared at me. I knew he was in great pain, and in that moment, I knew he saw me as the one causing the pain. My heart shattered. I am not sure it has ever completely healed.

I remember that over the days following surgery, I lay in bed with Cameron much of the time. They put pink sticky stuff on his head, around the incision site, and I remember very gently pulling it out of his hair while he slept. He would wake up on and off and talk to us. It seemed like he was getting better. But then he had to have a second surgery a couple of days after the first one. In the first operation they had pulled out a big piece of tumour, but a small piece was left behind. The tumour was like the letter C. Removing the large piece left a void, and the small piece dropped into that space. They had to go back and get it. They didn't take very long, about two hours. They just opened up his skull and got that one piece. Dr. Singhal was pleased with how things went. But when Cameron woke up from the second surgery, he hardly moved. And he didn't talk. He didn't talk again for what felt like three months, but it was actually about six weeks. The second surgery was April 14. He sat up on Mother's Day, May 10. He winked for the first time May 18. He talked for the first time May 23, and he whistled May 31. He walked for the first time since the second surgery on June 7. Those milestones came so slowly. The doctors kept telling us that Cameron would walk and talk again, that what was happening was common, normal. It didn't feel common or normal. It felt like hell.

I don't remember being with Cameron when he woke up from his surgeries, but I must have been because I wouldn't have been anywhere else. It felt like we were in the hospital for years.

Kim: Cameron's mutism and inability to walk were side effects of the kind of tumour he had—we just didn't know it yet. And even when the clinical team explained it to us, Shawna and Jim—all of us—were terrified that Cameron would be the one person who never talked again.

I don't remember when they told us it was cancer. I know that Jim tried to prepare me for it, but I didn't want it to be real. And I don't remember if it was between the first two surgeries. But I do remember being in Cindy's office. (Cindy was the clinical nurse specialist on the oncology service.) She gave me a stuffed bear to hold when I went into the room where the doctors were waiting. I had a death grip on that bear. When the doctor told us that Cameron had cancer, I remember screaming "No" as loud as I could. Cindy said it was good that I screamed. Wishful thinking makes me want to remember her saying she wished more people would get their feelings out, even if it meant screaming.

Kim: I was in the room when the doctors told Shawna and Jim that Cameron had cancer. Shawna screamed and screamed. Jim held her until the screams stopped. Then she pulled away as if sinking deep into herself, and she quietly sobbed. Over the weeks in the hospital, Shawna would go to the parents' shower room, get under the pouring water, and scream until there were no more screams for that day. Then she would dress for the day and go back to Cameron's room, composed once again, always with a smile

*on her face. I could do nothing but watch and hope that this ritual helped
her bear the weight of caring for a very sick child.*

Once the doctors knew that Cameron's tumour was cancer, he had to
have a spinal tap. They needed to see if cells from his brain had migrated
to other parts of his body. I remember being terrified. He had to lie still,
so at the doctor's request, I held him down. I was so angry at them for
making me do that to him. It was a painful procedure, and I was afraid
that Cameron would be mad at me because I let them hurt him. Another
time they gave him a suppository because he was constipated. It was so
invasive and distressing for him. Removing his catheter after surgery was
another traumatic moment because they couldn't get it out. Two female
nurses were pulling on his penis, but it still didn't come out. Finally a
male nurse came in and removed it in two seconds. Cameron's intense
desire for privacy emerged while he was in the hospital and never went
away. And he was a free spirit before he got sick, open to new experiences even though he was often shy at first. His experience in the hospital
changed all that. He retreated and became cautious. He is still cautious
all these years later.

*Kim: The staff tried very hard to respect a child's privacy, but it wasn't
always possible. And no explanation is really good enough when you are
five. Cameron was a compliant patient for the most part, but he often looked
very distressed when the nurses headed his way. He was never sure what
they were going to do to him next. I don't think he trusted any of the adults
around him except for the lady who took him to the playroom.*

When we were discharged, we didn't go home. Cameron needed to
have radiation daily at the BC Cancer Agency, but it was done on an
outpatient basis. We lived about an hour's drive from Vancouver, a long
drive each day. So we moved into an apartment in Vancouver instead. I
was disconnected a lot during that time. I was with Cameron all the time,
but I don't think I was being a very good mother. I was so scared of failing
him; I wanted to stop feeling, stop feeling anything. I don't think I gave
Cameron as much attention as he needed. I shut down a lot, and Jim took
over. I think that's a lot of why we are where we are now. It opened the
door for Jim to start to exert more and more control in our relationship. It

set a pattern of behaviour between us that has never ended. Even though we are divorced, I can still feel that control, that pressure.

After Cameron's six weeks of radiation, we headed for home. I was starting to be able to handle more of Cameron's care. I was the one who took him for his blood work. I was there when the therapists came, and I did his feedings. He had to be fed through a feeding tube. If he threw up his feeding tube, I dealt with it. However, I don't feel like I did a very good job; I could have done so much better. There was so much more I should have done. I could have been more engaged with the therapists. Maybe I could have tried harder. But honestly, when they came over it was my chance to not be the mom of a kid with cancer. So I treated them almost like babysitters instead of people actively trying to improve my son's life.

I don't think that I was ever afraid that Cameron was going to die. But I was very worried about the toll that everything we were doing to save his life was taking on his little body. I wasn't even that worried about the side effects of the chemo. I knew that there was some concern for his kidneys and some concern for his hearing. But when Dr. Goddard (the doctor who administered the radiation) told us about the possible side effects of the radiation, I was scared. Radiation was going to do the most damage. It was the thing that was going to cause him to have learning disabilities. It was the thing that was going to make him stop growing. Who he was before surgery wasn't who he would be in the future because of the things we had to do to keep him alive. That's what scared me the most. And yet, I kept thinking, "He has to live, he has to outlive me. He has to become a grown-up. That's all that matters." In the normal way of the world, children outlive their parents. I didn't want to outlive my son.

Outside of our family circle, my friend C was the biggest help. She never let me get too serious about everything that was going on in my life. She would pinch me (not too hard!) if I started to cry—it was her way of hugging me. And she had a dark sense of humour. She took what was happening and pushed everything to the extreme—she could be silly. She made me look at things from that silly angle. She made me laugh all the time. And we talked—about Cameron or about other things. We just talked. It really helped. One night she and two other friends from work came to visit me—it was really late. We sat outside on a picnic table, smoking. Cameron had been in the hospital for about ten days, but it felt like years. Being with them was good for me; it reminded me that there was an "outside"—that there was still a world carrying on without us. The rest of the world kept turning, but we were in a bubble separate from it. And we'd need to re-enter it one day. Talking with my friends helped me keep a bit of balance.

I don't have a lot of memories of those first months after Cameron was diagnosed except that it was a hard time. I was very lonely. I remember that I didn't know how to act, what to do. If there was anyone else around, I would relinquish Cameron's care to them. I didn't believe I was doing the "right" things for him, whatever that meant. I thought, "Good, there is an adult in charge, and I don't have to do this care anymore." I didn't think I was "good" at caring for Cameron. I went back to work part-time after about four months, and that was a helpful distraction. I was good at my work, and since I didn't feel any good at caring for Cameron, work was an opportunity to feel that I was proficient at something.

I don't think there's anything I would or could have asked of others. I had to "do" for myself. And even if I'd had every human on the planet around me all the time, telling me what a good job I was doing, that I was succeeding and doing a wonderful job, that I was a great mom, it wouldn't have mattered. I wouldn't have believed anyone. There wasn't anything for me to ask for.

As time went on, I did start to feel better—I got more comfortable with what Cameron needed from me. I got much better at handling the medical requirements of his care. I am not sure if that was because I was back at work and had responsibilities or if it was simply the passage of time. In an odd way, things were very regular. Thursdays were either chemo or blood work. Fridays were recovery if it was a chemo week. We had a routine that I was responsible for, and I felt comfortable, capable of doing what I needed to do. This went on and on for eighteen months.

I remember moments, small things, from the time Cameron was sick. I made a bracelet for him. Every bead represented something that had happened to him—chemo, radiation, blood test—each had their own colour. I still have it. And I have the doll that Child Life gave Cameron the day before his first surgery. He was meant to colour the doll, but he didn't get it done before they took him to the operating room.

Kim: I had worked at Children's Hospital years before Cameron got sick. In fact, I had been a Child Life specialist, a part of the medical team that helped prepare children for tests, procedures, and surgeries like the one Cameron was about to have. I knew Cameron's nurse, so she asked me to use that doll to help explain to Cameron what was about to happen. She thought it would be nice for Cameron if I helped him with the doll. But they came to get him for surgery early. I had just started to tell him what was going to happen in surgery, but there was no time to explain how he would feel after. As they wheeled him out of the room I was shouting in my head, "Wait, not yet! He isn't ready. I am not ready." They took him anyway.

Cameron had six weeks of radiation, one treatment a day, five days a week, and then began chemotherapy. I wish I had taken a more active role earlier when Cameron first started having his radiation treatments. He had to wear a special mask and I couldn't watch them put it on him. I stayed while they gave him the anaesthetic but then I had to leave—I just couldn't be there and watch them put him in the mask. But things changed when he started chemo. When getting chemo was more of a routine, I would sing to Cameron while he got his IV started (we called it his poke). I felt like I was doing something helpful. When we hung out in the playroom, I felt like I was being a good mom. We played and made things. I felt like I was interacting with him in a way that I hadn't been in the earlier days.

I am not sure that the other parents around me knew any more than I did, but I was pretty intimidated by a lot of them. Part of that is just me—scared of other humans. They seemed to be very relaxed and confident. Even if they didn't know what they were doing, they looked like they did. I couldn't pull that off to save my life. I was actually quite scared to make friends, and I didn't want to share how I was feeling. Maybe life would have been easier if I did share how I was feeling, but I just didn't want to. I felt like I turned off my emotions, and being scared never went away. I disconnected. It was like I was in a bubble, watching everything that was going on around me. Home or hospital, it didn't matter where I was. I was scared. And I felt alone most of the time. My feelings were often dismissed by my husband and that left me floundering. Why were my feelings less relevant than other people's? Without being able to talk about how I was feeling, I withdrew. It was my defense mechanism. If I wasn't really *there*, it wouldn't be so upsetting. If I was all the way *there*, I would feel all the things I didn't want to feel.

Kim: I would try to be with Shawna and Cameron on chemo days as an added distraction. It was fun to be in the playroom with them. From the time Cameron could hold a crayon or a glue stick, he and Shawna would do crafts of some kind, always making decorations for every event. Presents for grandparents, cards for teachers. It was their way to be together. This pattern continued in the hospital, and it became, once again, a way for them to stay close, to normalize a situation that was out of their control. There is nothing "normal" about being five years old and spending every other Thursday in the hospital with a needle stuck in your arm. Crafts saved those days and brought happiness for a while to a boy and his mum.

There were a couple of things that did help me during the time Cameron was getting chemo. The first one was making a binder, a planner where I could write down appointments, mark chemo dates with butterfly stickers, keep track of Cameron's blood counts. I needed to be able to see everything in one place. I am a linear thinker, so the binder was perfect. My advice to someone else with a sick child is figure out what makes your thought process calm down. If you are like me, get a binder. If you are a mind-map person, use mind maps. Do whatever you need to do to calm your brain so that you can process everything that is going on around you. I still have the binder.

The second thing that was so important was having an advocate for me, having a person who was "my person." My person was S, the clinical nurse specialist on Cameron's team. She gave me the idea for the binder. I don't know if that was what she did for every parent, but it was what I needed. She was there every time we went to the hospital, so if I had questions or concerns, I could ask her. She was kind and she was detailed—just the combination I needed. Cameron had different nurses caring for him as well, and they were all wonderful. And he had K, the Child Life specialist, who focused on his specific needs. But I had S, who focused on me.

Like C, most people tried to be helpful, but there were a couple of people who did things that were not helpful. For instance, the manager I had at the time showed up at the hospital just after Cameron's second surgery and told the staff that she was my sister. She was an Asian woman, probably twenty years older than me. It is hard to imagine that anyone would believe she was my sister. Without asking me, the nurses let her in. She thought it would be a good idea to come and wait with me. It wasn't a good idea. It might have been okay if we got along but we didn't. I couldn't believe she would do that, and I yelled at the staff for letting her in. It was so intrusive and entitled of her to think that I would want her, of all people, in the room with me while my son was recovering from surgery. C had told her specifically not to come. And yet, there she was! No thinking person would have arrived unannounced and unwanted, especially after being told not to come.

My mother-in-law wasn't always helpful. In the beginning she was supportive. She would have Cameron during the day while I was at work and would sometimes keep him for dinner so I could have some time to myself. But slowly her presence became more intrusive. She would come to our house uninvited and do things that I didn't ask her to do. More damaging was her undermining me with Cameron and with my husband.

Jim began to make more demands as well. For example, he wanted me to keep the house tidier. When I asked Cam to clean up his toys, or even if I tried to put them away, my mother-in-law would tell me I was being too strict, so I would leave the toys where they were. Then Jim would come home and be angry because the toys were still out. I tried to tell him what his mother had said and that I was upset about her interference. Then I would just cry. Jim told me that I didn't have a right to be upset with "other people" (his mother), even if they were interfering, because "they were having a hard time too." I was supposed be grateful she was helping. I wasn't. I felt very alone. All the time.

I would like to say that I became a stronger, more confident person sooner because of the experiences I went through when Cameron was sick, but it's not true. I was just as terrified. All the time. Completely useless. I eventually got comfortable doing what was required for Cameron around his treatments, but I don't think I ever turned into the kick-ass confident mother that he deserved. I wasn't an assertive woman, standing up for her son when he was sick. I was terrified at the beginning and I only got just a little bit less terrified as time went on.

Jim and I would have separated eventually, even if Cameron hadn't got sick. It just would have taken longer to get to that point. But Cameron being sick pushed me to see that I didn't want to be there anymore. I needed to be out of that house and out of my marriage. I thought, "I am so miserable. I have to leave to be alive for my son. If I stay, I am going to die." I literally wouldn't have survived the darkness that my marriage had become. I had deferred to Jim on everything for so long that I wasn't sure what I could do on my own. When I left him, I had to do lots of new things, things I had never done before, and I did them. For example, I had to rent an apartment, but they only accepted paperwork by fax. I didn't have a fax machine, so I had to go find a store that did—I paid them, and they faxed the rental agreement. That was weird but I did it anyway. I had to buy all the furniture. I had to rent a truck to move stuff. And I did it all. Finally I got to do whatever I wanted. That was really important to me. It was literally the first time in my entire life I could do anything I wanted to do, and no one was going to challenge me. I could leave a pile of papers on the other end of the couch for weeks and tidy it when I felt like it—not because of the looks and comments I was getting, but because I felt like it. I didn't have to consult on anything. Meals, furniture, where I went, how long I was out, the colour of the walls. It was nobody's business but mine.

I found peace and contentment in my new life. There were large chunks of time when I was happy. It was so satisfying to strip the ceiling in my kitchen, rewire the lights in my living room, tile my bathroom. I did things I had never done before, and it made me happy to know I could do anything I put my mind to. Cameron's illness was a trigger, the catalyst for me to become the grown-up I am today.

For me, resilience means getting up every day and doing what needs to be done that day—I don't connect being resilient to feeling confident or powerful. I connect it to putting one foot in front of the other—get up, breathe. Or get up, throw up, breathe, and then do what I have to do that day. Resilience doesn't automatically make you confident, sure of yourself. It means I got up today and did what I had to do. And I have done that every day. There are still days when it's hard, and I'm ever hopeful that resilience—being resilient—becomes second nature. I had to take care of myself. It was easy to let other people take care of me, but when I was on my own, I had to learn. There was a pride in knowing I could take care of myself. I learned I could do anything I had to do to take care of myself and my family.

I have spent years trying to inspire Cameron, to help him have his own voice and thoughts, to help him want to be independent. I still try and push him. I am his cheerleader. And maybe, just maybe, my resilience will light the path for him to embrace his own resilience.

Kim's Reflection

Shawna told me about moments when her inner resolve helped her through difficult periods in her life, but she acknowledged that until we talked, she hadn't thought of those occasions as a demonstration of resilience. In fact, she adamantly rejected the idea that she was resilient. When I pointed to times when she had shown great strength, she pushed back, claiming that they were simply moments when she had to "get on with it." Slowly she came to see that "getting on with it" was a fundamental part of being resilient.

Some people bounce back quickly from adversity; others take time, but they get there. Like Liz, Shawna's resilience was a slow burn, a flicker of hardiness. Shawna didn't think of herself as resilient because, like many of us, she hadn't needed to look for that characteristic until Cameron got sick. She had hit bumps in the road of life, and some of them knocked her sideways, but she had always found a way forward, a new "right" path. However, none of them had prepared her for Cameron's diagnosis. Shawna froze the day the doctor said the word "Cancer." For a time she didn't see how she would cope. But then slowly, with much thought, she began to redefine how to live in the new paradigm.

When I read Victor Frankl's words about finding meaning in your life, I thought of Shawna. Frankl said, "We must never forget that we may also find meaning in life even when . . . facing a fate that cannot be changed" (p. 10). Shawna had her meaning. Cameron was the "why" in her life. She didn't want him to be defined as "the boy who had cancer."

Shawna's initial steps forward meant taking control of her own life so that she could take care of Cameron. That is what Frankl meant when he talked about facing the reality of the current situation. Only after that step could you begin to look for a new meaning for life. Shawna's first step was figuring out how to care for Cameron as they navigated the uncertain days cancer presented them with. The next step was ending her marriage. It took courage to leave and begin again. Without knowing it, she was following the path Frankl laid out for finding meaning in the new order. She had no choice but to reframe what life would look like because everything had changed. She made the decision to move away from what felt like a perpetually grey world, and instead find a place where there was sunshine. It took time but she did it. The life Shawna has today is the result of the resilience she demonstrated in the early days of Cameron's diagnosis.

Anxiety has been a challenge for Shawna for many years. The source wasn't always clear and that left her with an unsettled feeling that perhaps the feelings weren't real, or that she shouldn't feel the way she felt. It was confusing and frustrating. But she knew that feeling anxious about Cameron was very real, and in an odd way that experience legitimized her ongoing struggles with anxiety. She was afraid for Cameron and that was real. She faced her realities, as suggested by Frankl and Stockard, and like them, she didn't lose hope. Learning how to manage her anxiety differently has been a silver lining in the hunt for resilience.

Shawna has a family who loves her and friends who care deeply for her, but that was not enough to propel her forward in the early days of Cameron's illness. She had to go into herself and find a hidden reservoir of strength. She had to figure out how to build the new life by herself. She needed to do life her own way if she was going to fulfill her dream to help her son find his own resilience as he grew to be a man. She couldn't rely only on other people to build a new life for her and Cameron. Was she successful? I leave the final words to Cameron:

"My mom is a good mother. She is always there for me. She is kind, caring. She helped me become the man I am today by allowing me to grow my independence."

CHAPTER SEVEN: JUDY

Kim's Story

JUDY AND I MET AT *a Mums and Tots group in 1982. We were both new to Vancouver, and this group was a way to meet other women with small kids and, for a few hours, escape being just a mum. It didn't take long for us to build a friendship that went far beyond the group meetings. We just clicked! Judy and I had that special magic between us, and it has continued for over forty years. We have stood beside each other as our lives have unfolded. There have been ups and downs aplenty. We have laughed, cried, been angry, made up—you name it, we have experienced it. Our families grew up within the circle of our friendship.*

Judy comes from a large family, and she has many friends. People are drawn to her as I was those many years ago. Her sense of humour, her dedication to her family, her belief in the goodness of mankind, and her deep faith in God have created a unique blend of Wonderful. There is one more key ingredient that completes Judy, and that is her husband, Greg. Judy and Greg have been married for over fifty years. It is difficult to describe their relationship without sounding sugary and perhaps a little glib, but they are a team in every sense of the word. They are each other's best friend, and no matter what has gone on during any given day, they wait for each other. As the lights dim, they are together. Fifty years is a long time. They have mellowed, edges have softened, but the love just keeps getting stronger, deeper.

Greg was hospitalized for a day in May 2017 while visiting their son in Toronto. He had lost his memory for several hours, and the doctors ran a number of tests. The tests didn't give them any explicit reason for the memory loss, but one of the tests showed a small growth of some kind in the back of his brain. The doctors didn't think the growth was creating the memory problem, and they weren't concerned about it. They suggested he follow up with his own doctor when he returned to Vancouver. Greg had more tests when he got home. The growth turned out to be a tumour, and his doctor referred him to a surgeon. The tumour was removed; it was benign. Everyone gave a sigh of relief.

Greg recovered more slowly than he expected but still, life was good. His business was flourishing, his kids and grandkids were doing what they were supposed to be doing. Judy was finding new outlets for her own creativity. And then the doctor called. Greg's one-year checkup showed that the tumour had returned.

Judy and Greg had faced many hurdles over the years, but nothing prepared them for what came next.

Judy's Story

When I look back over the last two and a half years, I see time in four parts, four seasons. The first season included Greg's original diagnosis and surgery, the recurrence of the tumour, and his second surgery on November 2, 2018. The second season was the time Greg spent in ICU, from November 3, 2018, to February 15, 2019. The move to Maple House on February 15, 2019, began the third season. And then the fourth season—COVID-19.

Greg and I went out for dinner on November 1, 2018. It was Greg's last dinner before he went into surgery for the second time, to remove the new tumour in his brain. Our thirty-two-year-old son, Blake, and his girlfriend, A, were with us, and we had a lovely evening. Little did we know that it would be the last dinner like this that Greg would ever eat. Forever. Greg felt that the surgery would go well and he'd be back to work in a few days. I was more apprehensive. I had this ominous sense that it was not going to be great, and I just wanted to relish the time together, have a nice memory of a nice evening. Later, we went to bed, and like every other night, we prayed together. We prayed that this surgery would go as well as the last and our lives would continue on a normal path.

We got up early the next morning, got ready, and headed to the hospital. Blake and A and my sister Gale came with us. I took a picture of Greg going into the hospital. I remember him standing there as I snapped a picture of him. It was dawn, a beautiful morning. As I took the picture, this big wave of fear came over me. It is hard to describe. I took another picture of him smiling at us just before he went into surgery. And then we waited. We knew the surgery would be several hours. Friends came by with a big picnic lunch for us, which was a lovely distraction.

Finally, the surgeon phoned me. He said, "The surgery is over, and Greg is in the recovery room. You'll be able to see him in about an hour." I asked how the surgery went and he said, "The surgery was successful." I went back to let everyone know what the doctor had said and that we would be able to see Greg soon.

In an hour I rang the recovery room buzzer and a nurse said to come back in half an hour. When Blake and I went back, they said to come back in another half hour. I was starting to wonder what was going on. Finally, Blake rang the buzzer for the third time. A nurse came to the door and said, "Before you come in, I have to tell you that Greg is not recovering from the surgery the same way he did from his surgery last year." He walked us across to Greg.

Greg was hooked up to every imaginable machine, but he was awake. He looked horrid. And he said, with really slurred words, "My worst fears have come true. I'm paralyzed."

I said, "Honey, I'm sure you're not paralyzed. You have had brain surgery and I think it's just the effects of the anaesthetic."

He said, "I know I'm paralyzed." His tongue was almost hanging out and he looked horrific.

I repeated what I had said about just coming out of surgery, but I was really thinking, "What the hell has happened?" Within a couple of minutes, the nurse told us it was time to go. I didn't want to leave but I had no choice.

Blake and I left the recovery room and walked down the hall toward my sister and Blake's girlfriend. Blake collapsed into A's arms, weeping. Gail hugged me, and as she did it was as if I went into shock. My right leg was flopping on its own, moving up and down. I sobbed. Gale took me outside to the small courtyard near the recovery room. I remember just trying to breathe. I knew I had an Ativan in my purse. A dug around and found it for me. I was embarrassed at what a mess the purse was—funny what odd things you think about in the moment and what you remember later.

I kept asking, "Why would the doctor say the surgery was successful?" It clearly hadn't been. I said, "I don't think he's paralyzed but he looks horrible. Really horrible. And I think he had a stroke."

A couple of hours later a nurse came and told us that they were moving Greg to a ward. This was good news because it meant his condition was more stable. I thought to myself, "Things will be okay." Blake had brought me a coffee just before the nurse came. Greg loved coffee, so when I got to his bedside, I teased him, saying, "Do you want to smell it?" We were trying to be light and upbeat for him. But things were changing around us. There was a quiet buzz in the room, and we could hear the nurse's voice but not what she was saying. She was on the phone, and the next thing we knew a nurse from the Intensive Care Unit (ICU) arrived and was checking Greg. At this point, nothing had been said to us about Greg's condition. Suddenly the buzz got bigger. Everyone had to leave the room except for me. The nurse told me Greg had to the ICU because he wasn't breathing on his own. In an instant his condition became a much more complicated issue. Once again Greg was on the move, and I was left behind. His nurse told me I would be able to see him in a couple of hours. He was on his way to the ICU, and I was on my way to wait. Just wait.

Finally they called us to the ICU. When we got there, they told us that Greg was paralyzed. They explained that he would never walk again and probably never eat or drink on his own. All I could think about was how serious the situation was. Greg was now a quadriplegic. And I wondered, "How in the world did this happen? How did we end up here, like this?"

We went home quite late that night. I remember Blake lying face down on the floor, sobbing, listing all the things his dad would never be able to do again and all the things he wouldn't ever be able to do with his dad again. I was so worried for Blake—he was broken. And I was in shock. It was a very long night.

My second season began the next morning: ICU. Words like *horrific, overwhelming, traumatizing, astonishing* washed over me. There was my beloved man, who walked into the hospital believing he would be out in a few days, lying helpless. Everything we knew was completely reversed.

In those early moments I decided that I would be strong; I would do whatever needed to be done to help him through this. I began to educate myself. I learned medical terminology, and I researched the implications of Greg's condition so that I could speak intelligently with the medical team, ask good questions. I had to trust the doctors, and at the same time I learned to be an advocate for Greg. Learning everything I could about Greg's condition was the only way I could be the advocate he needed.

I had to tell our family and friends what had happened and deal with the shock everyone was feeling. It was exhausting. Even now I run into people who don't know what happened to Greg. When they ask, "How is Greg? I haven't seen him for a while," I take a breath and tell our story again. And again.

A few days after Greg was admitted to the ICU, a young doctor came into the room, rolling a cart with his computer on it. He was a bit of a cocky fellow and it felt like he was excited to give this lecture to us. He asked, "Do you want the bad news first or the good news?" I'm not sure we answered him quickly enough because he simply began to talk to us. I remember him telling us, "The bad news is you are a quadriplegic. And there is a little more bad news for you. The tumour is going to grow back, probably within a year, and it will choke the life out of you, and you'll die. The good news is that you're in a good place where we can care for you." He was very thorough, including a description and pictures of what parts of Greg's brain were dead. I wanted to ask him questions, find out what part of the brain was okay and what could happen. But I didn't know what questions I could ask, or which I needed to ask. Both Greg and I were so stunned by this young doctor's approach that we were left speechless. The whole discussion was shocking.

Three or four weeks later they confirmed that Greg had in fact had a stroke. I kept saying from the beginning that it looked like he'd had a stroke, but no one would confirm it. It was so frustrating. After more breathing tests they also confirmed that Greg would require a ventilator for life. Worst case scenario. His doctor wanted to do a second surgery to see if he could do something to help Greg breathe on his own. I was sure that Greg would die in surgery. But as I waited in the hallway during that surgery, I saw a stretcher go by and I shouted, "Those are Greg's feet. He is alive!" Everybody thought I was crazy. But it was him, and he was alive.

I honestly was stunned that he had lived through the surgery. But the operation didn't help, and it caused a bleed that required a third operation a week later. Each surgery was exhausting for Greg, and each time I thought he would die. I was exhausted too. More exhausted than I had ever been in my life.

Over time I formed close bonds with the ICU staff. The experience we had with that young doctor in the first days didn't happen again. The staff were very kind, very understanding. It was a good team. I felt supported and I trusted they would protect Greg. We had so many questions—Will Greg improve? How much will he improve? Will he come home? If not, where will he go? Greg wanted to come home and I wanted him home if possible. But we had months ahead of us in the ICU before Greg would be ready to go anywhere. Having the loving support of the staff made life a tiny bit easier to face each day. It was such an intense place, and I was there every day for many hours.

The other thing about the ICU is that it is the ICU; in an intensive care unit, anything can go wrong in an instant. I was on high alert—terrified—all the time. I would arrive at the hospital already tired from the drive. Then I had to find a parking spot, pay for parking, and walk to the hospital, almost always in the rain. Then came the long walk to the doors of the ICU. "What will I find today?" echoed in my head. "Is today the day he dies?" One day early on in our ICU stay, I was sitting in the waiting area when one of the nurses came and sat with me. "There you are," she said. "You know, Greg is probably not going to make it out of ICU. You have to be prepared." And I said that I didn't know that for sure, but I expected it. I didn't know what else to say. Over the next months, at least six, maybe eight different nurses took me aside and told me the same thing: I had to be prepared for Greg to die. So every day as I walked toward the doors, I wondered: "Is today the day he dies?" Or "How do I make him feel better?" Or "How do I pretend that things are getting better?" Or "How do I keep myself from falling to my knees?" It was gut-wrenching to see the man I loved lying helpless.

I drove to and from the hospital in the pouring rain throughout November, December, January, and February. There was just darkness. It was my faith that kept me going every day, my trust in God. I don't know how many times your heart can break, but in those months in the ICU my heart broke over and over and over. And it still breaks every day. Every day.

Miraculously, the time came when the doctors decided Greg was stable enough to move out of the ICU. He wanted to come home more than anything else, so I talked to the clinical team about bringing him home. I said that I would do everything I could to make that happen—renovations, special equipment. Whatever it took. I was in "get it done" mode—anything to make my man happy. But the whole clinical team was clear with me: taking Greg home would crush me. They said, "We are more worried about you than we are about Greg right now. Caring for him at home would destroy you, and we won't let that happen to you. Greg must go to a facility where they can care for him. He will require specialized care, and this kind of care can't be done at your home." Greg was very dependent on me, and they said if he came home, I would be on duty twenty-four hours a day, even if we had a house full of caregivers. It was difficult for me to hear what they said, but there was relief as well. That was a very hard day for me.

The only viable option for Greg was a place called Maple House. It had twenty-two beds dedicated to residents with ventilators. However, they were full. The only way you get into Maple House is when a resident dies. This meant that Greg could possibly be in the ICU for many more months. It was discouraging for both of us.

But since Greg would be going to Maple House someday, I wanted to see the place for myself. It was one unit in a large building called Fleetwood Manor. I asked the clerk at the desk in Fleetwood Manor if I could go into Maple House. I said that my husband was possibly going to move there, and I wanted to see what it was like. She said, "Sure, just go through those doors." The first person I met in the hallway was a nurse, Sunit, and she was one of the wonderful people who would eventually care for Greg. She showed me around, giving me an image that I could use to describe Maple House to Greg. Both Greg and I were excited at the thought of this next step but cautious because we didn't know how long we would have to wait.

In the end, it was a short wait. Greg moved to Maple House on Friday, February 15, 2019. The move to Maple House was the beginning of my third season. The staff from the ICU gave him a wonderful send-off. The nurses dressed Greg in regular clothes for the first time in three and a half months. They brought in a big heart-shaped pillow that all the staff had signed. And it was hard, so hard, for me to say goodbye to these people. They were my friends. The team had created such a protective bubble around us. I thought, "This is the ICU. This is where he's getting the best care." As we left the hospital, all I could think was, "Boom—now he is going out there to die." The words "to die" reverberated in my head.

When we got to Maple House, I sat on the couch, looking around, while the nurses settled Greg in his room. I wanted to vomit. I kept thinking, "This is wrong, this is so wrong." I didn't feel good about Greg's room; it had a weird vibe. He had to share his room with another resident, which meant we would have virtually no privacy. Once again everything was new, different. The staff asked me to leave at 5:30 so they could begin to familiarize Greg with his new routines. It was probably the worst night of my life. I felt I had abandoned him. As I drove away from the building, I kept thinking that maybe I should have pushed harder to bring him home. I felt I was leaving him with a group of strangers who didn't know him or love him or understand him. I knew he was frightened. I felt dirty inside, like I had thrown him away. I pulled my car over about four times to sit and bawl my eyes out.

That's probably the first time I got mad. I didn't have time to get angry before. Everything was so chaotic and intense in the ICU, and I was on such a steep learning curve. In the hospital there were so many things to learn, like how to operate the wheelchair, what to do in case of an emergency. So many things. But I was also surrounded with a caring team, and I was connected to other families who were going through a similar experience. My time was full, and even though everything was intense, I felt supported and so did Greg. Then suddenly I just dropped him off at a strange place—with no ICU support team—and drove away. I hated it. I hated it. I just hated it.

In the hospital, I had to be Greg's voice, his representative. In the beginning, the staff didn't know him. He was just a guy who came in hooked up to equipment, who couldn't breathe or talk. I needed them to know Greg, to know he was a good man and that he was loved not just by me and the kids but by many people. Over time the staff did get to know him as I did, and they too came to love him. I enjoyed representing Greg—it was part of my contribution to helping him get better. I felt like I was part of his care team.

Maple House was completely different from the ICU. After the hospital chaos, this environment was immediately peaceful. There was gentleness in the air. So my insides shifted from feeling traumatized by this new move to trying to accept the change. I say *trying* to accept because I really had not fully accepted what had happened to Greg in the first place. But the daily chaos gave way to a quieter routine. The first three months at Maple House were difficult, but when Greg was moved into his own room, we had the privacy we both yearned for. He was happy in his room. There was a big window, and he could watch cars coming and going. He had his own TV. I could read to him. We could talk. We had the privacy to just be together. Our family and friends came to visit, and the next months were a more settled period. I got to know and love the staff. In many ways they have cared for me as well as Greg. They have laughed with me, and they have held my hand while I cried. Greg had three near-death episodes, and each time the staff handled both Greg and me with love and respect.

When I look back on those early months spent in the ICU and then in Maple House, I wonder if I should have been further ahead emotionally. And yet I am not sure what that would have looked like. I was grieving the loss of the man I married, but I was finding it very difficult. I could only go to a point and no further because Greg was still alive. And I was so thankful that he was still alive, that he was still cheerful. I had so much to be grateful for, and yet I felt such deep sorrow. No more sleeping together, no coffee in the morning, no stupid jokes about a song we heard on the radio. So many wonderful memories of our life together were intertwined with what we had now lost. I was so sad whenever I thought about the future that we had imagined. But then I would stop myself and think, "What is the point of thinking about what might have been?" Instead I had to think about what life was going to be now.

Why wasn't I angry? Why couldn't I just get very angry about what had happened to Greg's life—to my life? I wondered if it was my self-control. Did I have to control myself so much that I couldn't howl like I did that first night after Greg's surgery? Was I still in shock, or was I too afraid to let go? Was my faith enough to carry me through? I asked God for help, and maybe his help was to ease the anger. I asked myself these questions, and many more, all the time. Questions went round and round in my head.

I think Greg accepted his situation more than I ever did. I didn't want his life, my life, our life, to be the way it was now. I wanted to crawl in through the window and rescue him, put him in the bottom of a laundry cart and haul him out. It got complicated in my head. I tried to grasp the new reality and live with the fact that Greg was dying. He had a tumour that was going to choke the life out of him. He had also developed a heart condition that could act up and kill him. But even though Greg was most often realistic about his circumstances, there were times when he believed he would recover, and it was his hope for recovery that got in the way of my anger, pulled me back, renewed my own hope. I cleared some things out of his office, but I didn't give them away. I put them in the garage because Greg believed he was coming home, and what if he did? What if there was some freaking miracle—what if he came home and I had thrown his things away?

Greg was a contradiction; he could be sharp and clear in his thinking one moment, then living in a fantasy the next. One of those fantasies involved planning a road trip. As much as his hopes and dreams often short-circuited my grief, listening to him describe the trip was like having a dagger thrust into my heart. I knew it would never happen. And so reality and hope battled each other in my head. It baffled me.

I have learned many things about myself since Greg's first surgery in 2018. I learned that I could do anything I needed to do, from talking to a brain surgeon to cleaning the hair out of the drain of the bathroom, re-caulking the shower, or selling our business. I learned I could run a household on my own. I was always compassionate, but that compassion, that empathy, went to a deeper level. I learned to not care so much about circumstances I couldn't control. I've learned that other people's problems couldn't become mine because I had enough of my own. I can quickly make a decision about whether I need to help or just let it go— *that's not my problem*. I always tried to fix things for everyone, but I've learned I can't fix everything.

I've learned to really trust God, more than I had ever done before, and a lot of that came from Greg. When the doctor told us about the second tumour, we were stunned. I said to Greg, "How are you feeling?" He replied, "Really afraid." I said, "Here's the bottom line. We can either live in fear, or we can trust God, but we cannot do them both at the same time. So every time the fear comes, we are going to have to make a decision." We both said, "We're going to trust God." That decision helped a lot. When I was overwhelmed, Greg would look at me and ask, "Judy, who's in control?" I would say, "God." Then he would ask, "Who do we want to be in control?" And I would say, "God." I already had a deep trust in God. Perhaps I just embraced that trust more. And perhaps this deeper trust helped me in ways I didn't understand when I was angry and grieving.

Over the years, Greg and I dealt with difficult things in our life with humour. We would just pick up and go on. We didn't spend a lot of time sitting with hurt or sadness. But now I've learned to stay in this hurt mode for a longer time. I've learned how to feel the pain. And I'm very sad about the situation, sad about where we are now, sad about the loss of the life we had. Intensely sad. Heartbroken again. Still.

I am surprised by how easy it was to do all the hard stuff. It's been exhausting. I have had maybe two dozen days where I thought, "I just don't want to do this anymore," but most of the time it's easy. I'm surprised when people tell me how much they admire me for doing this "amazing thing." I don't think of it that way. I'm just loving my husband, and that is easy.

There isn't anything that I would do differently. I truly feel I have given everything to this. I have been there for Greg. I pulled up every resource I could for him. I managed his friends and his hundreds of visitors. I managed my kids the best I could, helping them cope with what happened to their dad. I didn't feel I could let them know how I was really feeling, and that was probably to my detriment, but I didn't want them to worry about me, to lay my sorrow on their shoulders. I have stood beside my man, done what needed to be done. I have no regrets.

If I met someone going through a similar tragedy, I would encourage them to let people help them. And whatever faith or God you believe in, whatever's "out there" that helps you, really embrace it. Also, understand that some people don't know how to help. Whatever they try to do, thank them for it. And if you need something, ask for it. I learned to accept all the help that came to me. In fact, I was overwhelmed many times by the lovely things people did. Food, flowers, hugs. So many wonderful outpourings of love. I let them know how much their gestures of kindness meant to me. And there were stand-out moments of generosity, like the friend who came and sat with Greg all night every night for six weeks when he was afraid to go to sleep. So many things like this overwhelmed me.

There were unexpected gifts along the way, and things I learned because of Greg's situation that I never would have otherwise. The first gift was the friends I've made at Maple House. I talked before about how, in the ICU, I had a group of people—nurses and others—who supported me. They became my friends and then I lost them when we left the ICU. But new friends were waiting for me, for us, at Maple House. The staff welcomed us, creating a new bubble of love. Most of the staff are East

Indian, and they have taught me so much. They introduced me to a new culture, and I am so grateful for that learning. I have come to know and love the staff, and they have come to know and love us.

The second gift was that the medical staff, visitors, and new friends came to see my Greg the way I saw him. In his life before surgery, he often appeared very businesslike. He was quiet in big groups, an observer more than a participant. His hobbies were solitary ones. He rode his motorcycle, flew planes, and, above all, he loved cars. His quiet nature was perfect for his work in insurance. People trusted him implicitly. He touched many people over the years, but this was different. These people all saw my real Greg, the Greg I lived with every day for fifty-two years. I loved that—I really did.

I missed Greg's physical presence in the house. I think we always had something special. He could drive me crazy sometimes, and no doubt I could make him crazy too. He had his quirks, just like I have mine. But I always really loved his physical presence, right from the minute he walked in the door every day. When he got home, he would search me out. He always made me feel like I was valuable, the most important person in his life. He really loved me, and I knew he loved me. We joked a lot; our life was full of humour and laughter. I miss that. I was thinking this morning that I am not very funny anymore. He was so darn funny! We would laugh at the stupidest stuff. But not only was he not in our home anymore; he couldn't even stand up and hug me, and I missed that physical touch. Whether he was in his bed or his chair, he was separate from me.

In March 2020, COVID-19 arrived, and with it what I think of as the fourth season, the fourth phase, in the whole process. The precautions required because of the pandemic meant Greg and I spent only a few minutes a day talking to each other, because we had to talk through a glass window. We talked on FaceTime, but it was in short bursts. I wasn't doing anything interesting because I had to stay home, and Greg was certainly not doing anything exciting. We were running out of things to talk about. Suddenly it felt awkward between us for the first time ever. Before the virus hit, I would spend hours with him. We talked and laughed all day about all kinds of things. People would come to visit, and that gave us more things to talk about. Then it all stopped.

I really struggled with the COVID-19 restrictions. I cried a lot. And I wonder if isolation was actually good for me because I was forced into a quiet time. Perhaps I was meant to work through the myriad of feelings swirling in my mind. I worried all the time about Greg dying. And I wondered if this fourth season was a way for me to pull away from him so that when he died, there was already some separation. I missed Greg more than I had in the three years since he became sick.

Sunit, the first nurse I met at Maple House, became one of the very special people in our life. On one of the nights we thought Greg was dying, she took me in her arms and held me. My lips touched her neck and I thought, "I just want to stay here forever." I was aware of a deep connection with her. I think I was so weepy during the pandemic because the nurses were my friends, and I couldn't see them. I made close connections with this new care team at Maple House. I saw them every day for over a year. They were my new friends, and suddenly they were gone. I couldn't see Greg. I couldn't see the nurses. I felt very alone. It was a hard time. So hard.

What did I love about my "new" Greg? He sat in that chair for months, and yet he was grateful. Grateful to be alive. I don't think he complained more than three times about anything. He spoke up if he had an issue, but he did not complain to me about being in that chair or his circumstances. It was not what I expected of him. The night before surgery we talked about all the things that could go wrong, and he said, "I do not want to end up in a wheelchair. I would rather die than be in a wheelchair." And there he was, in a wheelchair. He did say, "I'd like to die because I don't want to be a burden on you." He didn't say he wanted to die because he was in a wheelchair.

I was dumbfounded by his acceptance and by the way he inspired other people. I had dozens and dozens of people, maybe 150 or 200, say to me, "I was so afraid to go and see Greg. I thought I would be devastated, and I came away inspired. In the end I feel better about life." I'm very proud of him for that.

My resilience, my strength, comes from a few places. My dad always told my brothers and sisters that we could do anything. He would encourage us, telling us to try, just try. And so we did. He believed in me and so I believed in me.

The second source of my resilience is my faith. I know I am not in control of what is happening to Greg, and I believe that God will take care of us. Despite all that has happened, Greg and I trust that God will care for us as we are meant to be cared for. Everybody dies, and when God calls Greg home, that's His plan. If, miraculously, God allows Greg to be healed, then that's His plan and I get to ride along with it. That acceptance gives me great strength.

The third and critical area that feeds my resilience is how I have been carried on the shoulders of my friends. There were times when I was getting sixty to eighty messages a day from different people. I don't think Greg and I had four days all to ourselves without visitors. Cards still come in the mail. That continuous support feeds my inner strength in ways I never thought about before, because I didn't have to.

I have learned that I am deeply loved. And I am strong. I am okay.

All things work together for good
For those who love the Lord
And are called to His Purpose
Romans 8:28

Greg died on June 1, 2020. It was peaceful, just Greg and Judy, together. As it was always meant to be.

Kim's Reflection

Loss isn't new for Judy. She has lost her parents, a brother, and, over the years, a number of close friends. Her kindness and generous spirit have been a haven of comfort for many. And those events always reminded Judy about the fragility of life. But when you are married to your best friend and lover for fifty years, losing that person is incomprehensible.

It has been just a little over a year since Greg died, and the veil of deep sorrow is slowly beginning to lift for Judy. There have been many days filled with tears. But something else is happening too—Judy has begun the process of reclaiming her life, exploring who she is now without Greg. Like Frankl, Stockdale, and others who have gone before her, Judy faced the reality of Greg's situation, and her own. And like them, she is finding new meaning, new purpose in her life. Judy faced her new reality every day for two years. There was no place to hide, no place to pretend that life was not drastically altered. But she didn't back away. As Frankl said, you have to accept the cruel reality, but for a long time Judy had no hope, nothing to make meaning of. How do you do that when the person you love is going to die soon? Instead she made a different kind of meaning and found a different kind of hope. Judy made Greg's altered world the best world it could be. More importantly, she was fully present each and every moment. The meaning making and the hope were squished into the small room where Greg lived, but it was a room filled with love. That was how Judy flexed her resilience muscles.

Katy Hutchison is the author of Walking After Midnight, *a story about her journey after her husband died. She wrote, "I learned that you do what you need to do when faced with life challenges. There is an eerie calm in the eye of the storm. It is a place where, if you listen to the whispers of your own heart, you are able to gather together your courage, and you cope. What comes into play are the hidden life skills that you possess and may not even be aware of" (ebook). Those words echoed in my mind when I read them because that is what Judy did. For months, in spite of the unpredictable nature of Greg's illness, Judy was calm. She found the whispering sounds in her heart that Hutchison talks about. And now Judy is using that same courage to figure out how to move through sorrow to the other side. That is resilience.*

I don't believe that grief goes away. It may soften, the edges may blur, but it doesn't disappear. It travels with you. I see Judy's grief in her eyes, hear it in her voice, but I also see her strength and her deep faith edging her forward. And Greg's spirit sits gently on her shoulders, reminding her that she is strong. Now she believes it too.

CHAPTER EIGHT: GREG'S STORY

In the previous chapter, Judy talked about the traumatic event that changed her life. Her husband, Greg, was diagnosed with a brain tumour that took away his ability to walk, to breathe on his own, and so much more. Judy described how she dealt with the many changes brought about by this traumatic event, and she explained what she learned about herself because of the many trials she faced.

This chapter tells a different side of that story. It describes the time I spent with Greg after he moved from the hospital to Maple House. It is the story of what I learned while I sat beside him, and how he became the inspiration for this book. These are excerpts from the journal I kept during the time I visited Greg.

GREG AND I HAD BEEN social friends for forty years. He always had a cheerful word, a helpful bit of advice, or a silly joke to share, but my deep friendship was with Judy. I was devastated when he was diagnosed with the tumour, but my attention focused on Judy. When Greg survived his surgeries and was moved to a care facility, I knew that Judy would need a different kind of support from me. I asked her if I could visit Greg each week, giving her a few hours to tend to errands. She accepted my offer, and I began to spend every Wednesday afternoon with Greg. I had no idea how my friendship with Greg would blossom or that he would teach me so much about resilience.

I didn't visit Greg in the early days of his time in the ICU. I talked to Judy regularly, asking if she needed anything from me, hoping she didn't because I was too scared to go to the hospital. I didn't want to see the new Greg. Cowardly behaviour. But after a few weeks I finally went, and I kept going.

Four months later he was still alive and ready to leave the hospital for a care facility. It was a place for people who, like him, were compromised beyond their wildest imagination. Greg's courageous spirit got him to this next step, and I wanted to be part of this chapter of his life.

SPRING 2019

Today is my first day alone with Greg in his new room at Maple House, a unit in the care facility he now calls home. When I came last week, Judy showed me the ins and outs of Greg's setup—what I could do, what I couldn't do, and, most importantly, when to call for help. This was all essential information, but none of it lowered my anxiety. And now I am here, sitting in my car, looking at the building, preparing to go in and be alone with Greg for the first time. Finally I get out of my car and go to the door. The woman behind the glass wall shouts "Hello" and pushes an invisible button. I walk in, sign my name in the guest book, wash my hands with antiseptic solution, and walk towards the unit where Greg lives. As I approach his room, I hear the quiet whir of machinery keeping him alive. Without that gentle sound, he dies. "So really," I think to myself, "how gentle is that sound?"

Greg sits in his wheelchair, dressed in regular clothes—except they aren't regular clothes. Someone has created a business for themselves making clothes for people like Greg who live in a wheelchair, people who can't dress themselves. I can hardly see the snaps and Velcro holding the pieces in place. He looks presentable, tidy, just like in his other life. Except this isn't that life. Many things have been systematically stripped away. Destruction in the wake of the scalpel. No more walking or eating, no working, no driving, no flying. No sex. It is an impressive list of "can't do that anymore."

Greg sees me and smiles. He reaches for my hand and kisses it just before a spasm takes over his grip and my hand is unceremoniously flung aside. I brush my fingers through his hair, kiss his forehead, and ask how he is doing. He moves his fingers in a motion that tells me things are okay. Not great, but okay. And I play along. But nothing is really okay, is it?

I read to him; we watch TV. And we talk. I have a ready list of questions, some mundane and others probing. On this day we discuss the upcoming Canadian election, both of us laughing at the crazy shenanigans that seem to permeate every election.

There is a short lull in the conversation, and then an abrupt shift as Greg begins talking about medical assistance in dying (MAiD), the option he has, with the support of his physician, to choose when to end his life. It is a legal process in Canada. He says that he and Judy have been talking about MaiD. Greg tells me that they have decided to keep it as an option, but that he isn't ready to make any final decisions. "Life seems good," he says. "It is there, if and when I am ready."

As Greg talks, I grow more and more anxious. What should I say? I don't understand where his desire to live comes from, and I wonder what choices I would make if I were stuck in this room. Murmuring the occasional *hmm* seems the best I can offer. The word *coward* pings inside my head yet again. Slowly the conversation veers away from that topic, and I breathe a quiet sigh of relief. Silence once again fills the room and that is okay.

Then I ask, "How did you meet Judy?" He smiles and his eyes light up. His eyes always shine when he talks about Judy, and this day is no exception. He says he met her at the A&W, a hamburger joint. He knew about Judy because his friend lived down the street from her. "Judy thought I wanted to date her friend Gail, but I had my hopes set on Judy. And I brazenly made my wishes known. That was it—we have been together ever since—fifty years."

Greg says she is his special weapon. "The first impression you get of Judy is how nice, how cheerful she is. And that is true, but sometimes people miss how strong she is, how clear. Fierce. She is my secret weapon." *Just like you,* I think to myself. *You are her secret weapon too. Kind and funny. Fierce.* His love for his family knows no bounds. His children bring him great joy. But Judy, well, she is his sun and his moon. She understands him. Their marriage is one that has been built on a bedrock of trust and love. And humour. She makes him laugh and he makes her laugh. They have been a formidable team. He needs his secret weapon more than ever before.

The Maple House staff care for Greg with gentleness and kindness. And in return he guides them. They are the medical specialists, but he is a human specialist. Or humane specialist. He told me that one evening there was a new nurse, a young woman, looking after him. When he rang his bell, she came in and stood at the end of his bed asking, "What do you need?" He said he looked at her for a moment and then said, "That isn't the right question. Ask me what I want. Or ask me how you can help me." He then said, "When you ask me what I want or how you can help, it feels like you see me as a person, not just a patient." He needed her medical expertise, but more than anything he wanted her to see him as a person first, a patient second. Hard to explain, easy to understand. Instantly the young nurse understood. She reframed her question, and as she was leaving the room, she turned to Greg and blew him a kiss. She learned a critical lesson that night: look for humanity first.

Greg tells me about a few lessons of his own that he has learned along this new path. He managed his old life like a well-oiled machine. Fastidious doesn't begin to describe how Greg approached life. Things in their place, lined up in a specific, orderly way. Cars shiny, tires rotated, coffee hot, hair short. Bills paid, garage swept, motorcycle shiny. Now he must wait—wait for his turn. There are twenty-some other people just like him in Maple House, also waiting their turn. Waiting doesn't come easily for Greg, and I see the frustration in his eyes. It leaks out through the spasms in his hands and legs. My inclination is to jump to attention whenever he needs or wants something. Fix. Do. Call. Repeat. But not so fast. I watch Judy and I applaud the graceful dance she does with Greg. She is teaching him a new way of being, of behaving. He doesn't have control of everyone, everything. Her patience is becoming his patience. Such a difficult shift when you are almost seventy! But this is where love comes into play; that special language they share slips into the front seat of their new existence.

So now he waits. Or at least he tries. He was a very successful businessman; he flew airplanes; he rode a motorcycle; he was a pillar of strength in his community. People relied on him for many things, but those pieces of his life all went away. Now he is adapting to his new life, and he is doing it with the same intensity and integrity that he has always done everything, and he is pulling strength from his deep well of resilience. He is trying to accept this new reality and find the purpose within this unfamiliar landscape.

When I arrive on Wednesdays, there is often someone visiting Greg, usually a male friend from his work or his church or perhaps a neighbour. As they prepare to leave, Greg reaches for them and kisses their hand, telling them he loves them. The gesture is received with some uneasiness but always with gratitude. After one of these occasions, Greg reveals to me that he tells everyone who visits that he loves them, especially his male friends. He says he knows it might make some uncomfortable, but he does it anyway. He doesn't mind if they squirm; he says he wants them to know he cares deeply for them, that he really does love them. I know what he means because sometimes I squirm! But we all kiss him goodbye in spite of the squirm because we can't not. It is his gift to us. This is a new gesture for Greg. He didn't tell everyone he loved them as they walked out of his office, but now it is critical to him that everyone knows how he feels. Our gift to him is acceptance. He is teaching us that life is too short, too unpredictable, to let discomfort get in the way of saying "I love you." Trust the love. Accept the gift.

Greg has few illusions about being anywhere other than in Room 180. And he is okay with that, most of the time. He says, "It is beautiful here. Look around. The staff care about me, and I have so many visitors. I think over four hundred people have come to see me. And I think they come because I tell them I love them." I agree. And I wonder, "Where does this strength come from? How can he see beauty in his new life, the one where so much has been stripped away?" It is easy to be resilient when life is moving along smoothly, but what about when that smooth life disappears?

Greg lived an orderly life before he got sick. Friends would tease him about his meticulous approach to everything. Now the need for outward

157

order is more important than ever, and he gets frustrated because he can't help himself. He gets agitated if the sheets on his legs wrinkle or his glasses are smudged, or the curtains are not open evenly. He just can't do anything about it himself. Now he must ask for help. And that is where we, the visitors, come in. The gift of order comes freely from all who grace his presence. I can't make his body work properly, I can't make his hands behave, but I can close a drawer, smooth a blanket, accept his kiss, and believe him when he says, "I love you."

Greg is a Christian. When he became a Christian, I was very sceptical about what it all meant. In the early days he was what I expected—zealous. But as the years passed, I watched his faith deepen, moving away from zealotry and simply becoming a part of who he was. Greg was always a good person, a kind person, but slowly a new, deeper layer formed. His faith added a layer of character that I see clearly as I sit beside him in Room 180. His courage in the face of this catastrophe comes from a deep well of faith inside him. That is where his resilience is coming from.

AUTUMN 2019

One day I say, "Can I ask you a question?" He shrugs his shoulders and nods. I ask, "What has surprised you about how this year has unfolded for you?" I'm not sure what I am hunting for, but I think that we can begin with the word *surprise*. He starts talking about the people in the facility, how he prays for those who landed unexpectedly in this place like he did, hoping that his prayers will help them. But then he shifts his focus and talks about the staff. This isn't a new topic but there is an urgency in his voice. He talks about one nurse in particular, a beautiful nurse from a country in Africa, who asked him one evening if she could pray for him in her native language. He smiles when he talks about her, about her kindness, her gentle demeanour. He says that he was surprised by her wish to give back to him that which he had given to her: the gift of prayer. He says he was surprised to see how there was so much life happening inside the walls of this institution and that he felt it was his calling to share himself in any way he could with everyone around him, especially the staff. And share he did! Kindness, laughter, and, most importantly to him, prayer.

Nothing is okay about the loss of who he was, but he is showing each of us who enter his room that his life is still worth living. He believes he still has something to learn and something to teach. He says if he didn't believe that he would have taken the assisted dying option. No one would blame him. But he isn't ready.

As soon as I walk into Greg's room on any given Wednesday, I want to know how he is feeling. And when I ask how he is, he tells me the truth. If it is a good day, he says so. If he is down, he says so and we talk it through. His voice is often soft, and it can be a struggle some days to get sounds out. There is a gravelly quality to the words. His vision is often blurry, and his energy can drop quickly. But every time I arrive, he is glad to see me. Our time is dictated by him. I know the TV schedule by heart— *Wagon Train, The Rifleman, Bonanza*. We both love *Bonanza*! He doesn't like the idea of horseback riding and neither do I. We both admit that we are more than a little afraid of horses. He doesn't like to have dirty hands; he waves his hands in the air and makes a face and his message is clear. And we agree that sleeping on a mat in the dirt doesn't look like fun. The biggest takeaway for both of us? We would make lousy cowboys!

Another *Bonanza* moment sparks a conversation about ironing. I say I love to iron. Greg looks at me and smiles. "Me too." We both start to laugh because we know there are those who love to iron and those who think we are nuts. At a deeper level, it reminds both of us of something he can't do anymore, and yet we can laugh in that instant about our crazy love of a wrinkle-free world. It is a lovely memory.

On days when he is tired, I sit quietly and let my mind wander. On one of those days, I think about independence. As adults, we believe that we are independent creatures, free to make decisions for ourselves, to care for ourselves, do as we wish. But as an inmate of any kind of care facility, the notion of independence is challenged, revised, and for some, like Greg, removed entirely. How we adjust defines how we move forward. Greg must be listening in to my thoughts because he begins to talk about the damage the stroke caused, how the nerves he had never given any thought to are now broken, how he is at the mercy of others. I say that the loss of independence must be devastating, so shocking, to realize that you no longer have control over your most private activities, relying on others to take care of not only the big things like breathing, but the most personal as well. He agrees with me. He has accepted that this is his life now and being angry isn't going to get him anywhere. He says, "If I am angry all the time, who will visit me?" I am reminded that our health care teams need to be vigilant in ensuring that a patient's dignity is protected whenever possible, that dignity isn't a casualty of medical care.

Greg pauses for a moment and then begins to talk about Judy. She is his favourite conversation topic. He talks about their closeness, about his love for her. He says one of his nurses asked him about his relationship with Judy, asked where their love came from, how it grew. He was a little taken aback by her questions, but he did his best to answer. She asked if he could find her a husband, one like him. He smiled and shrugged. He wasn't sure he could! Then she paused, leaned in, and asked if he felt a flutter in his chest when he saw Judy. He smiled and told her, "Yes, every single time. Even after fifty years." As he recounts this story to me, tears glisten in his eyes and he says softly, "There is just Judy."

Then he turns his head toward me and asks what surprised me in the last year. I know he means surprises about him, about his situation. I think about that for a minute and then I answer, "Your room is calm and welcoming. I was scared at first. I was worried I would make a mistake, do something wrong, and you would be harmed. But slowly, that fear has gone away. Now I am just very glad to be here with you." He says, "Lots of people come to see me. Sometimes there are five at a time. One day we had, I think, forty." And I tell him, "They will be scared the first time because they won't know what to expect, but very quickly they will lose that fear, just like I did. That is because of you and Judy. You are so welcoming; your warmth permeates this room. Whatever fears people have slip away and they are free to simply be here with you."

I didn't know how to answer his question at first, but the longer I thought about it, the easier the answer was: the space is like a sanctuary, a sacred space. Even the staff feel it. They drift in and out even when there is no specific reason to be there. And he loves them; he loves when they visit him for no particular reason. He talks with those young people about whatever is on their minds. His honesty and clarity, his gentle demeanour, and his sense of humour are the attraction. And he believes that building those connections is his work, his new calling in life. In his book *Man's Search for Meaning*, Victor Frankl talked about finding purpose in the face of tragedy. Greg found his purpose.

All that had been stripped away during surgery uncovered a new calling for Greg. He shows everyone who enters his room that life is filled with surprises—not all good, but then we choose how to take what we are given. We can either let the new unfold with light or dwell in the murky grey of despair. Greg chose to go into the light. And everyone who comes to visit sits in the calmness of Greg's sacred space. As one man said, "I receive more from Greg and Judy than I can possibly give to them. I feel better when I leave than when I arrived. It isn't scary anymore. Or not so scary."

Then I have another thought about what surprised me. Judy and Greg seem so in tune with each other, as if this crazy turn of fortune brought them even closer together. I say to Greg, "It is as if the distraction of your old life slipped away, and your ties to each other are now stronger, have grown deeper. Your love is more visible to me. Does that make sense?" He says, "Yes, that is true. We spend more time together than ever before." They talk about the necessities, of course—sale of the business, changes to wills, a Do Not Resuscitate order in place. But then the real stuff comes forward. They talk about what meaning this life holds now and how they will live each day together. One day I asked Judy if she needed an extra break for a day or two; if she did, I would come and be with Greg. She thought about it for a minute, and then she replied that maybe she needed a break—probably she did—but really, she just wanted to be with Greg. The catastrophe that landed them in this room has not dimmed their love. In fact, truth be told, it has renewed it. Surprise!

"What have you learned about yourself this year?" I ask. Greg says, "I have learned to be calmer, not to think about myself so much. To think of others first. And I have dug deeper into my faith, gone back to my faith. To read my bible. To listen to sermons on my iPad." And I think, "That is my learning for the day. I can be calmer. I can focus more on others, less on me." A reminder to have faith, live fully, and always put kindness first. I am one of those visitors who always receives more than they give.

One week in November, Greg is taken to the hospital because his heart is beating erratically. The doctors say he needs a pacemaker, but because of his perilous condition they can't perform the surgery. They tell Judy to gather the family because Greg won't last the night. The family begins to say their final goodbyes, holding him for the last time, loving him. But then Greg's heart rate begins to climb, to beat more steadily on its own. His blood pressure rises, slowly. The doctor, the nurses, and his family stand transfixed as Greg's body fights back. Within minutes he is laughing and teasing them. The doctors tell Greg his heart is struggling, but he knows for that day he is alive. Is his resilient nature part of the fight? I think so. He still isn't ready for a final goodbye.

WINTER 2019

When I arrive on December 26, Greg is in his chair, watching one of his favourite evangelists on TV. He turns when he hears my footsteps and gives me the best grin ever. In return, I give him the biggest hug I can, maintaining a balance between gentleness and outright exuberance. I haven't seen him since his second heart incident in early December. Once we get past the hellos and how are you, I sit for a moment just looking at him. He has his old glasses on. I ask why, and he tells me he is getting new lenses in his good frames. The doctor is hoping that new lenses will help stabilize his vision, which had been compromised by the stroke. "Fingers crossed," I say. And I think to myself, "He is still fighting."

I ask him, "Were you scared when you went to the hospital?" He shakes his head. "No, I wasn't scared. If it was my time, it was my time. But it wasn't." When he got back to the care home later that night, his nurse greeted him with a hug and said, "It wasn't your time tonight. You have more work to do." Greg took her comment to heart. He renewed his effort to make sure that every single person who came into his room left with the words "I love you" ringing in their ears. Family, friends, staff. Everyone.

In early January 2020 I arrive at Maple House on an unusually beautiful and sunny day. As I walk towards Greg's room, I wonder if the sun has permeated the space. But the curtains are closed when I enter, and Greg is sitting with his eyes closed. He is very still. At the sound of my entrance, he opens his eyes and gives me a wan smile, as if the weight of the world is resting on his shoulders. I kiss him on his forehead as he clutches my hand. He looks up at me with immense sadness in his eyes. "I am numb everywhere today," he says. "My hands, my legs, my feet. Don't tell Judy."

I take one hand and rub it gently. "Is this new?' I ask.

"Not really," he explains, "but it was better for a while. Now it is back. It is my spine." The nerves in his spine were severely damaged, and now the damage is slowly making itself known throughout his body. He wanted so much to regain movement, and any new sensation gave him hope. But today, that hope has slipped a little.

Then he turns the conversation away from himself and focuses on me. "What is new with you?" he asks. It is a deflection and that is okay. We both need a new conversation, so I regale him with stories from my week. Any story will do, just as long as it isn't about him. I always make sure I have some funny story up my sleeve, and today is no different. By the time I finish giving the news from my week, it is time for *Bonanza*. "Just in time," he says. One hour of distraction filled with cowboys and shooting, where the good guys always win. As the show comes to an end I wonder, "Why can't this good guy win?"

As I prepare to leave, I lean into him and kiss him goodbye. I say, "I will see you soon." He grabs my hand and, in a shaky movement, pulls me close. We are still for just a moment, and then I gently pull away. I wave and walk out the door. As I slide behind the wheel of my car, I take a deep breath. I think I was holding my breath for much of my visit. Sadness engulfs me and tears flow. I can go; he can't. Another day in Room 180.

On my next visit, I talk to him about my new writing project. "I am working on a new book," I say, "and I want you to be a part of it. It was inspired by you and our many conversations. You know that I write about you every day after we have been together. Now I want to make it more formal." I go on to tell him how I want to explore the concept of resilience in the face of instantaneous catastrophe. I tell him who else will be included and the format I have in mind.

He looks at me and says, "Are you asking me?"

I say, "Yes, I am formally asking you if you would be part of the project. I have already asked Judy and she said yes. Now I am asking you."

He smiles, takes my hand, and nods, and in his deep, whispery voice says, "Of course I will."

I take a breath and we move on. When it is time to leave that evening, I hug him, kiss his forehead, and we say our new goodbye mantra. Greg starts and I repeat: "Loved you then. Love you now. Love you forever." I am not sure if Greg says this to everyone, but it is always a special moment when he says it to me.

On the last Wednesday in February I bring Greg a small pink quartz heart and place it on his shelf amidst other bits people have brought him. I tell him the heart will remind him how important he is to me, and even if I'm not in the room, a piece of my heart is right there. He takes my hand and squeezes as hard as he can, lightly kissing my fingertips.

As I prepare to leave that day, we say goodbye the same as always. Hugs, kisses, and "I will see you soon." I cannot foresee that it will be the last time I sit with Greg in his room at Maple House.

SPRING 2020

In early March 2020 the whole world changed with the arrival of the COVID-19 pandemic. Everyone was in some form of quarantine. Maple House was shut to everyone but staff. No visitors, including Judy. I missed my time with Greg so much.

The last few visits before the pandemic arrived were spent in quiet conversations about daily life. Greg had come through some new ups and downs with his body. The nerve pathways seemed to be even more compromised, creating more twitching in his legs and arms. He was agitated, and his speech was scrambled from time to time. Was Greg beginning to lose his battle, was his time slipping away? I thought about all my questions and wondered if I would be able to ask them. He had always been so great at answering!

With the arrival of COVID-19, and the strict No Visitor policy, Greg lost his greatest joy—physical connection with friends and family. No more touch, no more hugs. Even the nurses had to wear gloves and masks. It just wasn't the same. In the early days of the pandemic, I would stand outside his window, calling to him. It was exhausting for him to respond, but we tried. However, even that kind of visit ended; no one was allowed within six feet of the building, making visits impossible. He had become so isolated.

Greg died June 1, 2020. Judy was with him, just the two of them. They started this journey together, and they ended it together. He had grown so weary over those last months, and now he was at peace.

Because of the pandemic, there was no large gathering where we could come together to celebrate and say thank you to Greg for all that he gave us. Hundreds of visits to his bedside, hundreds of kisses and "I love you's." We saw through the machines; none of us lost sight of the man. In spite of his predicament, he welcomed each of us and thanked us for our time.

Resilience is defined as the ability to cope, to adapt in the face of adversity and emerge stronger. Greg demonstrated his resilience every day. He showed us we can live until we die, and that dying isn't the most terrible thing that can happen. The event—the surgery, the illness, the death—may be cruel and punishing, but what you do after is what really matters. Greg lived the time after his surgery with a kind of grace that leaves me yearning for more of him. After every visit I asked myself, "What did he teach me today?" I was never disappointed.

In the two years between Greg's initial diagnosis with a benign brain tumour and his death, he fought to live. He was shocked at first, but he faced the first surgery with determination and the will to return to his robust, healthy self with as little delay as possible. When the tumour returned and he faced a second, more gruelling, surgery, he was frightened. The prospect of being incapacitated scared him. He told Judy that his worst nightmare would be to live, condemned to life in a wheelchair. The worst happened and he had to figure out what to do.

The will to live is a powerful thing. There were many times during Greg's stay in the ICU when he almost died but didn't. He fought and he fought; he wanted to go home. His spirit and inner grit kept him focused on that prize. When the doctors told him he couldn't go home, that it was impossible for Judy to give him the specialized care he needed, he was once again faced with the monumental question "Now what? How do I go on? Do I go on?" But he rallied, and together with Judy and the medical team, he began to look forward to the next hurdle. The stumbling blocks were difficult to accept, but each time one appeared, Greg found a way through the disappointment. His deep faith was a pivotal support. And his belief that life was still meaningful, precious, carried him forward.

As his physical world shrank, Greg's kindness and compassion for people around him expanded. His resilient nature opened him to everyone in a way that was different from the way he was before he got sick, and that was the gift he left each of us. His message was clear: Even in the darkest of times, there is light if you just reach for it.

I miss my friend.

Loved you then; love you now; love you forever.

Kim's Reflection

Greg was in the prime of his life when he was diagnosed with a brain tumour. That tumour was growing while he was busy living, loving, doing. After the second surgery, when the doctor told him he would never walk or breathe on his own again, Greg was devastated. He wasn't sure he wanted to live that way; he wasn't sure he wanted to live at all. There were days when he was overwhelmed and sadness crept in, settling in his heart. But then, from somewhere, hope broke through, and he looked forward, curious about life in this new, broken body.

Victor Frankl and James Stockdale could never have predicted where life would lead them. They faced catastrophic events that left them scarred forever. But in spite of those experiences, they survived because they believed their lives still held purpose. Greg followed in their footsteps. He faced the reality of his situation and then found new purpose for his life at Maple House. Surprise!

Greg's experience reminded me of Rick Hansen, author of Going the Distance. *Rick was fifteen when he was in a serious car accident that left him a paraplegic. He went on to become famous for his Man in Motion tour, a journey that saw him wheel around the world, highlighting what a person can do when they have a purpose. He said, "Every day . . . remember to ask yourself: 'can I dig a little deeper and pull something out that I never knew*

I had before?'" I believe that Greg lived his last year and a half at Maple House with that question in his mind. He opened himself up to everyone who came into his room, and he did that with one intention—to make sure they knew they were loved. He found an inner strength and purpose he hadn't tapped into before. Was it always there? Resilience scholars would say yes; he just needed to reach for it. And he did. He lived fully, with one goal, to the end. Every person he touched knew, beyond a shadow of doubt, that they were loved.

When Greg died, I searched for words to describe the man I knew, the one who said "I love you" to me every day as I left. Ralph Waldo Emerson gave me the words.

> *"To leave the world a bit better, whether by a healthy child,*
> *a garden patch, or a redeemed social condition;*
> *to know that even one life has breathed easier because you lived—*
> *that is to have succeeded."*
> *Ralph Waldo Emerson*

CHAPTER NINE: A FINAL REFLECTION

WRITING THE FINAL CHAPTER HAS been the most challenging of all. How to begin so I can end? What words will convey the magnitude of the gift of story my friends gave me so I could share it with you? How to sum up the resilience found in those stories of remarkable yet ordinary people, like you and me, who found themselves in extraordinary circumstances and made their way through grief to find a new, surprising life.

As a writer, I started with a glimmer of an idea that slid around inside my head for months, then slowly started to take form. I was not sure where this idea of resilience would take me, but I trusted it was important to share because that seed of an idea wouldn't go away.

Reading the definition of resilience wasn't enough for me. The definitions were all so vague. I wanted to step away from them and explore how people lived into their own resilient nature. I turned to the literature and read the words of people like Victor Frankl and James Stockdale, who lived through horrendous times only to find a new life. And people like Jim Collins, Diane Coutu, and Maria Konnikova who studied resilience for years. Then I turned to the people close to me, my friends, family, and coworkers, who had lived through a moment of instantaneous loss. They were not content to exist in the shadow of a former life; they found a way to live into the present. As a result, this book is a celebration of life.

It honours the intrepid spirit of each person you read about. They did not succumb. As Bindy said, "I still had a life, and I knew I had to go on."

So what were the surprises in all of this? One surprise was the willingness of the nine people to tell me their stories. Life recounted in story has the power to touch the soul, mend the heart, and shine light on the path forward. My friends did that for me and for you—and, in the end, for themselves. Not one described themselves as resilient, but as they told me their stories, said the words out loud, they saw what I saw—strong, resilient people. Another beautiful surprise!

To be resilient is not a passive act; it takes work. And resilient people come in every size and shape. Each story you read was deeply personal. Yet at the same time there were similarities between the stories, and themes that emerged throughout the book.

Before they found their resilience, the storytellers struggled with shock, fear of the unknown, and grief. They all talked first about shock, that first moment of complete disbelief, and their inability to respond. Liz said, "I couldn't cope with anything. It was like I was catatonic . . . I couldn't do anything except cry." As Judy watched Greg return from surgery, she wondered, "How in the world did this happen? How did we end up here, like this?" For each person, the shock of losing their old life in an instant was overwhelming. The question *now what?* reverberated over and over. In *The Year of Magical Thinking*, Joan Didion describes the visceral response she had to her husband's death: "The unremarkable moments just before tragedy changes everything—those moments are the clear ones. What follows those moments, well, they are not so clear. Everyone I spoke to knew what they were doing just before their world changed. Showering, driving, talking about the weather. Pretty much anything that goes on in a routine way is remembered. Then, the brain shuts down and for a time, stumbles, unable to recall the mundane. That is what happens when we are faced with instantaneous, life-changing moments." As Diane said, "I remember thinking, 'I don't know how to book a flight, to even get dressed . . .'" Shock can leave us incapable of the smallest, most familiar tasks.

Next comes fear—fear of the unknown and fear of the known. The path forward is shrouded in darkness, and what used to light that path is gone forever. Fear bumps up against shock, and the overwhelming question pushes in: *How will I ever cope?* When the doctor told Paul he had cancer he thought, "This is a place where I don't have any control of the outcome." Dodie's response was the same. She said, "Suddenly my whole life fell apart. Everything crashed . . . I realized that I couldn't control everything." How do you cope with these catastrophic changes when you no longer have the sense of control you had before? Liz asked: "How was I supposed to live this new life?" Few of us spend time thinking about *what if*? Loss catches us by surprise, takes our breath away, and leaves us searching for firm ground, a clear path, control.

Then overwhelming grief crashes down, peppered with anger. Diane said, "Everybody wanted to know how they could help, asking what I needed. What did I need? I didn't know what I needed. Except I needed my husband." And as Cameron was wheeled into surgery and the door to the operating room closed, Shawna said, "I turned, and I hugged my mother. She told me it was going to be okay. I yelled at her and I stamped my foot. I shouted, 'No, it is not going to be okay. This is not okay.'" And she said, "When the doctor told us that Cameron had cancer, I remember screaming 'No' as loud as I could." The impossible happens. There is no answer to *why me*?

Over time my friends learned to live with the grief, balancing it side by side with the new, unexpected life. This is a complex relationship, and Judy expressed the contradiction beautifully: "I had so much to be grateful for, and yet I felt such deep sorrow." Bindy said, "Laura's death was the worst thing that ever happened to me. And I learned how to get through it." And Liz commented, "You learn to live with [grief], and the pain eases, but it never goes away." Kate Bowler, author of *No Cure for Being Human*, had a conversation with theology professor Jerry Sittser about loss and grief on her podcast *Everything Happens for a Reason*. Sittser had lost his wife twenty years earlier, and he talked about the untidiness of grief. His comment made sense to me because grief is messy. We all hope that grief will pass quickly but that never happens. Diane laughed when she told me she decided one day to stop grieving. "I thought, 'Snap out of it girl, just get on with it.' So I decided—no more grieving. Check. Done. Except it had only been three months. How could I have possibly expected to just 'get on with it' after only three months?" Grief comes in crashing waves when you least expect it, and then it happens again and again. Sometimes the waves are small, but they still hit you. Dodie cried every time she went to the doctor's office. She said, "I was just such a mess." But she learned to accept that there would be days when she could manage the grief that came with the loss of her old life and other days when the reality of her situation would be overwhelming. Sittser reminds us that you "can't go back to 'Before.'" He "had to figure out how to live while grieving the loss." Chaotic. Untidy.

Each of the storytellers demonstrated traits that defined them as resilient by Frankl, Stockard, Kushner, and Coutu:

- Pragmatic — Face the harsh reality of your situation.
- Flexible — Find new meaning in a life that differs from the one you imagined.
- Realistic — Accept that you really can't control *what* happens, but you can choose *how* to respond.
- Optimistic — Believe that life will get better.

When Frankl was in the concentration camp, watching people around him disappear, he knew that his life was in the hands of violent masters. All he could control was his mind. So he began to imagine seminar presentations for classes he hoped he would teach one day. He couldn't control what the Nazis would do to him, but they couldn't take away his dreams.

Coutu said, "Facing reality, really facing it, is gruelling work." And then she reminded us that optimism is a fundamental part of resilience. The characteristics of resilience described by scholars surged and receded time and again for the storytellers depending on the moment, but those fundamental characteristics never went away completely. And as I listened to each story, I heard *hope* in their voices, trusting that even in the dark times, life would get better. Paul's comment summed it up when he said, "I really think it's neat getting up in the morning. When my feet hit the carpet, I think, 'Jesus, you know, this is really nice!'"

As I talked to each person, I began to recognize other qualities of resilience that Frankl and Stockard had not touched on, so I went back for a second look at the lists described in the "How to Build Your Resilience" programs I mentioned in the Introduction. They identified additional aspects of resilience that supported everything Frankl, Stockard, Kushner, and Coutu had talked about.

The first one was belief in self. My friends came to see that they were stronger than they thought. Sharon said, "I always thought I was a strong person, but I learned that I am stronger, much stronger, than I believed . . . Trusting my heart, trusting my intuition and that faith in myself, that was my resilient Self guiding me forward." Liz said, "There was something deep inside of me that wouldn't let me 'quit' or 'collapse.' Some kind of deep drive that propelled me into surviving and somehow dealing with this loss." In her book *Between Two Kingdoms*, Suleika Jaouad wrote, "I had no interest in existing as a martyr, forever defined by the worst things that had happened to me. I needed to believe that when your life has become a cage, you loosen the bars and reclaim your freedom. I told myself again and again, until I believed my own words: It is possible for me to alter the course of my becoming." Even in the depths of their darkest moments, the will to carry on, to believe in themselves, pulled these storytellers forward. In the face of his worst nightmare, Greg grinned at me and said, "Life is good."

A second theme was the importance of support offered by family and friends. Every person talked about how critical it was to have family and friends close by. Diane said, "I attribute so much of my ability to cope with adverse situations to the depth of friendships I have." Bindy commented, "I was so fortunate to have such a great group of friends . . . Everybody knew everybody and we cared for each other as if we were one big family." And Liz noted, "I had so much respect for the friends who were brave enough to be part of that circle of grief . . . the best thing my friends did for me—they listened." Greg smiled when I asked him about family and friends. People came to see him every day, to talk and to pray. Their visits gave him purpose. He said, "It is beautiful here . . . The staff care about me, and I have so many visitors. I think over four hundred people have come to see me." With arms wide open, those who cared about my friends stepped forward. Learning to accept the help was one more step toward integrating the *Before* and the *After*. And an additional group was added to the list of family and friends by almost everyone: the health care teams. Paul reminded me how very important this group can be when he said, "One of the biggest things that helped me move forward was the straightforwardness of my health providers." Judy agreed, "The staff were very kind, very understanding . . . I felt supported and I trusted they would protect Greg." Kindness and encouragement can come from many places.

A third theme mentioned was the role of faith, the belief in a higher power. Not all the storytellers talked about faith, but those who did, did so with passion. On a number of occasions, Judy said, "It was my faith that kept me going every day, my trust in God." While she questioned the depth of her faith, wondering if it was strong enough to carry her through, she came to a place of peace. "I've learned to really trust God, more than I had ever done before." And Greg told me, "I have learned to be calmer, not to think about myself so much. To think of others first. And I have dug deep into my faith, gone back to my faith. To read my bible. To listen to sermons." Like Judy, Greg felt a calmness because of his faith, and when staff asked Greg to pray with them, he did. Dodie reached into her faith as well. She said, "Being Jewish has been a support for me. My family is not deeply religious, but I have a great appreciation for the values of Judaism. It deals very well with death and mourning, placing loss in the context of the cycle of life." Others spoke of a different but equally powerful belief system. Bindy's comment touched on this idea. "[Laura's] presence was there in my beliefs, in my values. I'm not really a religious person or a spiritual one either . . . but I do believe in honouring people. Working as I did, caring as I did, was my way of honouring Laura's memory." Belief in self; accepting the support of family and friends; faith in God, Allah, a higher power, or, like Bindy, a belief in honouring people—these are also cornerstones of a resilient person.

Exploring the literature and talking with the storytellers about resilience led me back to my original question, the foundational piece for this book: where does our resilience come from? Are we born resilient or do we learn how to be resilient? As each story unfolded, the storytellers found the words to describe their resilient nature and where that resilience was rooted. These stories were another surprise for me. Some spoke about learning to be resilient from their parents and grandparents. Paul spoke about his resilience so clearly. He said, "My resilience comes from the past, my upbringing, my childhood, and the influence of my mother." Bindy talked about her grandmother as her role model. She said, "Grandma never let herself sink into self-pity . . . When I have been in difficult situations or going through tough times, memories of my grandma helped me through." Liz commented, "My mother was always nurturing and comforting. But she is also a fighter and a very strong person. She was the one telling me to pick myself up and get on with life."

Others believed their resilience came from within. There wasn't a specific person or group of people who taught them how to be resilient; they just are that way. Sharon is one of those. She believes that her resilience comes from "the belief that life is the journey, and the moment I am in is what really matters." She learned as a young woman to rely on herself. Shawna echoed Sharon's thoughts. She said, "I don't think there is anything I would or could have asked of others. I had to 'do' for myself."

When I started reading about resilience, I wasn't convinced that you could learn to be resilient, and then I saw that I was wrong. People can learn how to pull from their inner resources and become resilient. As Shawna reflected, "Resilient means getting up and doing what needs to be done—I don't connect it to feeling confident or powerful. I connect it to putting one foot in front of the other—get up, breathe." She added, "There was a pride in knowing I could take care of myself." And resilient people aren't always strong. Each storyteller agreed that their strength and resilience ebbs and flows. Dodie smiled at me and said, "How am I? I don't know." There were days when she resented the chaos cancer had caused in her life and then there were the days when she could "flip back and feel thankful that I have now lived past my seventy-first birthday." Up and down, up and down.

Susan Sontag, an American author and activist, wrote about an intriguing idea that she called *dual citizenship*. She said, "Illness is the night side of life, a more onerous citizenship. Everyone who is born holds dual citizenship, in the kingdom of the well and in the kingdom of the sick. Although we all prefer to use the good passport, sooner or later each of us is obliged, at least for a spell, to identify ourselves as citizens of that other place." When I substituted the word *grief* for *illness*, I thought of Judy. Although she had experienced loss before, Greg's death was catastrophic. Now she lives with life and death side by side. She is finding a way to live with two passports. Each storyteller lives with two passports; it is required when you live in the world of *Before* and *After*. Bindy's final words captured the essence of two passports when she said, "I still have tears of sadness in my eyes when I think about Laura, and I can have tears in my eyes when I think about things of beauty. They live side by side." *Before* and *After*, side by side.

The final surprise I encountered was about myself. As I wrote this last chapter, I realized I hadn't stopped even once to ask myself the questions I asked each of the storytellers. Suddenly it was important for the integrity of my work to sit back for a moment, put my notes away, and take time to reflect on my life, searching for my resilience. I am not sure many of us ask ourselves those fundamental questions—Am I resilient? And if so, how? Where does our grit, our inner strength, come from? But I learned these questions are worth exploring.

I have not experienced that instant of devastating loss like my storytellers. In my mind, my life moved along like most people's do: ups and downs, some small bumps, some not so small. However, the more I thought about the accumulation of those events in my life, the more I realized how over time they slowly stripped away who I thought I was, challenging my beliefs and values, and leaving me wondering, "What the hell just happened?"

I was adopted. The idea that I had been given away preyed on my mind, and I worried every day that it could happen again, that my parents would uncover some flaw in me that would result in banishment. What to do? Keep going, keep being the best I could be. Live with the hope that I would be okay. Additional childhood traumas left me with secrets I carefully guarded for years, believing that the incidents must have somehow been my fault and if I told anyone, especially my parents, I would be cast out of the family. What to do? Keep going. I married at twenty and believed with all my heart that this was a forever thing. Until it wasn't. And there I was, a forty-year-old woman dealing with the end of a dream. What to do? Keep going. My father died, the person whose love for me never wavered even though I feared it would. What to do? Keep going. My grandson was diagnosed with cancer. What to do? Hold my daughter close, pray for a miracle, and keep going. And in the midst of everything, I was diagnosed with an illness that would become a lifelong struggle to manage. What to do? Keep going.

Like my daughter, Shawna, I woke up every day, got dressed, and kept going. But I also embraced the joys life offered, the moments of laughter, the hands extended in friendship. Looking back, I see that even though I carried the burden of accumulated grief, I looked forward, believing in myself and repeating, "I can do this." I found my way to a new place, a full life. That was my resilience, burning deep within me. Surprise! I realized that I too am resilient, and it came from a combination of love given to me by others and my own belief in myself. As the American author Wendell Berry said, "Life itself demands life of me." I answered the call.

My storytellers told us what they did when their lives shattered and lay like shards of glass at their feet. They told us how their resilience helped them figure out what pieces of their old lives would fit into the new one and that it was okay to leave other pieces behind. They created new meaning for their lives. What will you do the day your life as you know it changes forever? Trust that you will go on. Accept the help and support of others. Revisit your faith, whatever that means to you. I suspect that, like me, you might surprise yourself and discover that you too are resilient. And when you find that resilience, Celebrate!

RESOURCES

BOOKS

Baldwin, C. (1994). *Calling the Circle: The First and Future Culture*. New York: Bantam Books.

Bridges, W. (2004). *Transitions: Making Sense of Life's Changes (2nd ed.)*. Cambridge: Da Capo Press.

Coles, R. (1989). *The Call of Stories: Teaching and the Moral Imagination*. Boston: Houghton Mifflin Company.

Collins, J. (2001). *Good to Great: Why Some Companies Make the Leap and Others Don't*. New York: HarperCollins

Corrigan, K. (2018). *Tell Me More: Stories About the 12 Hardest Things I'm Learning to Say*. New York: Random House.

Frankl, V.E. (2006). *Man's Search for Meaning*. Boston: Beacon Press.

Kuhl, D. (2002). *What Dying People Want: Practical Wisdom for the End of Life*. Canada: Anchor Canada.

Kushner, H.S. (2002). *Living a Life That Matters*. New York: Anchor Books.

Manguso, S. (2008). *The Two Kinds of Decay: A Memoir*. New York: Picador.

Remen, R.N. (1996). *Kitchen Table Wisdom: Stories That Heal*. New York: Riverhead Books.

Youngs, B.B. (1996). *Gifts of the Heart: Stories That Celebrate Life's Defining Moments*. Florida: Health Communications, Inc.

ARTICLES

American Psychological Association. (2020, February 1). *Building Your Resilience* [Electronic version]. Retrieved March 11, 2020, from the American Psychological Association website: https://www.apa.org

Cherry, K. (2022, March 20). *What is Resilience?* [Electronic version]. Retrieved May 21, 2022, from the Very Well Mind website: https://www.verywellmind.com/

Colagrassi, M. (2018, November 15). *Stockdale Paradox: Why Confronting Reality is Vital to Success* [Electronic version]. Retrieved March 21, 2020, from the Big Think website: https://bigthink.com/

Coutu, D. (2002, May). Organizational structure: How Resilience Works [Electronic version]. *Harvard Business Review*, 1-18. Retrieved April 22, 2020, from the *Harvard Business Review* website: https:/www.hbr.org

Duggal, D., Sacks-Zimmerman, A., & Liberta, T. (2016). The Impact of Hope and Resilience On Multiple Factors in Neurosurgical Patients [Electronic version]. *Cureus Journal of Medical Science*, 1-9. Retrieved April 22, 2020, from https:/cureus.com

Konnikova, M. (2016, February 11). *How People Learn to Become Resilient* [Electronic version]. Retrieved April 27, 2020, from The New Yorker website: https://www.newyorker.com/

Kravetz, L.D. (2014, July 1). *Super Survival of the Fittest* [Electronic version]. Retrieved April 25, 2020, from the Psychology Today website: https://www.psychologytoday.com/ca

Lonczak, H.S. (2022, August 7). *Humor in Psychology: Coping and Laughing Your Woes Away* [Electronic version]. Retrieved September 26, 2022, from the Positive Psychology website: https://positivepsychology.com/

Marano, H.E. (2016, June 9). *The Art of Resilience* [Electronic version]. Retrieved March 24, 2020, from the Psychology Today website: https://www.psychologytoday.com/ca

Rutter, M. (2012). Resilience as a dynamic concept [Electronic version]. *Development and Psychopathology, 24*, 335-344. Retrieved March 4, 2020, from: https:/www.cambridge.org

Sehgal, P. (2015, December 1). *The Profound Emptiness of Resilience* [Electronic version]. Retrieved April 15,2020, from *The New York Times Magazine* website: https://www.nytimes.com/ca/section/magazine

The Term "resilience" is Everywhere—But What Does it Really Mean? (2019, May 7). Retrieved April 15, 2020, from the Ensia website: https://ensia.com/

Zimmerman, E. (2020, June 21). *What Makes Some People More Resilient Than Others* [Electronic version]. Retrieved February 16, 2021, from *The New York Times* website: https://www.nytimes.com/